"Any book that seeks to make the love of the Mother of God more understood and accessible, as does this current volume, is highly welcome. We are indebted to both Joseph and Ruth for this fruitful way to meditate on the Chaplet of the Seven Sorrows of Mary, revealed first to St. Bridget of Sweden in the fourteenth century. The honor due to the Mother of God is revealed both in the promises of the Seven Sorrows Chaplet and in a revelation to St. Bridget's contemporary St. Catherine of Siena. This revelation to St. Catherine from God the Father is why books like the current volume are so important: 'My goodness, in deference to the Word, has decreed that anyone at all, just or sinner, who holds her in due reverence will never be snatched or devoured by the infernal demon. She is like a bait set out by my goodness to catch my creatures' (*Dialogue* 286)."

—Fr. William M. Watson, S.J.,
Author and founder of the Sacred Story Institute

"Dr. Joseph Hollcraft and Ruth Berghorst's book, *The Contemplative Chaplet of the Seven Sorrows of Mary* is a multi-faceted treatment of the rich historical tradition of Our Lady of Sorrows. A deeply moving and inspiring read, it is a feast for the heart and mind. This book is a vital gift to the Church destined to be a spiritual classic. Highly recommended!"

—Kathleen Beckman, Speaker and author of *A Family Guide to Spiritual Warfare and Beautiful Holiness*

Praise for *Contemplating the Seven Sorrows of Mary*

"Everyone who has accompanied a loved one in their suffering knows a little of Mary's sorrowful heart. In this beautiful devotional, you will be led more deeply into Mary's wholehearted love for her Son and for all of us in our suffering. There are so many riches in this book—including how to engage our mind and heart in contemplating these mysteries of faith, along with ways to apply the Seven Sorrows to our own suffering and the suffering in the world. I highly recommend it."

—Dr. Bob Schuchts, Founder of the John Paul II Healing Center and author of *Real Suffering*

"Consider the Fourth, Fifth, and Sixth Stations of the Cross: Jesus meets His afflicted Mother, then Simon takes the Cross from Jesus' shoulders, and then Veronica wipes His face. In such proximity, Our Lady must have witnessed the actions of Simon and Veronica. Not only did they bring relief to Our Divine Lord, but they also consoled the Immaculate Heart of the Sorrowful Mother. When the cross weighs heavily upon our shoulders, or the shoulders of those we love, we eagerly seek and welcome the consolations that come from the kindness of others. Rarely do we consider consoling the Heart of Christ or of His Mother. Praying the Chaplet of the Seven Sorrows of Mary brings comfort to those two Hearts, which seek and welcome such consolation. Dr. Joseph Hollcraft and Ruth Berghorst guide us through this powerful devotion, which promises us an abundance of grace in our present struggles and, more importantly, consoles the Hearts of Jesus and Mary."

—The Most Reverend Gerardo J. Colacicco, Auxiliary Bishop of the Archdiocese of New York

"So much more than an excellent introduction to the Chaplet of the Seven Sorrows (which it is), this treasure of a book provides a sound catechesis on prayer, redemptive suffering, and Mariology generally. Anyone and everyone will be encouraged and edified in their prayer life by reading it and putting into practice its guidance."

—Dr. John Bergsma, Professor, Franciscan University of Steubenville and bestselling author of *Jesus and the Dead Sea Scrolls*

"In this soul-stirring work, Dr. Joseph Hollcraft and Ruth Berghorst invite readers to delve into the sorrowful journey of the Blessed Virgin Mary. The book begins by tracing the history of the Chaplet of the Seven Sorrows of Mary, shedding light on why we should pray this powerful devotion. As a foundation to better meditate on Mary's Seven Sorrows, Joseph and Ruth then offer a vision of mental prayer with St. Alphonsus Liguori—brilliant and practical. The meditations on the Seven Sorrows are rich, and their suggested list of whom and what to pray for is inspired and timely. If readers of this book take its direction seriously, I believe it will save souls!"

—Dan Burke, President of the Avila Institute and author of *Spiritual Warfare and the Discernment of Spirits*

"Timely, deep, and powerful, this work is a balm at a time when the Body of Christ most needs healing. Basing themselves on St. Alphonsus, who contemplated the Seven Sorrows of Mary to grieve and find healing for spiritual wounds, Joseph and Ruth prove to be reliable guides through the wounds and sorrows of the Church today. Where the sword of truth pierces our hearts with Mary, we find all those difficult places where Christ is longing to meet us."

—Dr. Anthony Lilles, Professor at Saint Patrick's Seminary and author of *Fire from Above*

"The brilliance and originality of this book stem from its dual approach, thoughtfully combining Mary's Seven Sorrows with a modern societal issue and a corresponding patron saint. Skillfully woven throughout the book are the teachings, promises, and reflections related to the sufferings of Mary, as presented by St. Alphonsus Liguori. In the ongoing battle for souls, this book, along with the meditative chaplet of Our Lady of Sorrows, is crucial in the fight against Satan."

—Patrick O'Hearn, Author of *Our Lady of Sorrows: Devotion to Mary's Seven Sorrows for Children*

CONTEMPLATING THE SEVEN SORROWS OF MARY

Joseph Hollcraft and Ruth Berghorst

CONTEMPLATING THE SEVEN SORROWS OF MARY

A CHAPLET WITH ST. ALPHONSUS LIGUORI

FOREWORD BY DR. MARK MIRAVALLE

SOPHIA INSTITUTE PRESS
Manchester, New Hampshire

Cover design by Mike Fontecchio, Faith & Family Publications.

On the cover: icon of the Mother of God "Seven Swords," photo courtesy of Pepelia Anatolii Konstantinovich; background (74545479) © HorenkO / DepositPhotos.

Sophia Institute Press
Box 5284, Manchester, NH 03108
1-800-888-9344
www.SophiaInstitute.com

Sophia Institute Press is a registered trademark of Sophia Institute.

paperback ISBN 979-8-88911-168-9

ebook ISBN 979-8-88911-169-6

Library of Congress Control Number: 2024940868

Second printing

To Roberta Seibert:
Our Lady of Sorrows is with you!

—J. H.

To my Savior, Jesus Christ,
who has given me everything,
and to my parents, Wilbert and Madeline,
first teachers of the Faith

—R. B.

CONTENTS

IMAGE CREDITS

ii. *Mater Dolorosa*, by Carlo Dolci, ca. 1655, Wikimedia Commons, public domain.

v, 71, 83. All Saints Catholic Church (St. Peters, Missouri)—stained-glass, sacristy, Immaculate Heart detail, photo by Nheyob—own work, CC BY-SA 4.0, https://commons.wikimedia.org/w/index.php?curid=34226007.

84. *Presentation of Jesus in the Temple*, by Fra Bartolomeo, 1516, Google Art Project, Wikimedia Commons, public domain.

96. *Flight into Egypt*, by Rembrandt, 1627, Yorck Project, Wikimedia Commons, public domain.

106. *Christ among the Doctors*, by Bernard van Orley, ca. 1513, Wikimedia Commons, public domain.

118. *Christ Carrying the Cross*, by Raphael, ca. 1516 (E8F7DT) © Heritage Image Partnership Ltd / Alamy Stock Photo.

128. *The Crucifixion* (MNXWTW), by Titian, 1558, © The Picture Art Collection / Alamy Stock Photo.

138. *Descent from the Cross*, by Niccolò Frangipane, 1593, photo by Didier Descouens—own work, CC BY-SA 4.0, https://commons.wikimedia.org/w/index.php?curid=51752320.

148. *The Entombment*, by Giovanni Francesco Barbieri, ca. 1656, Wikimedia Commons, public domain.

FOREWORD

To ponder the Seven Sorrows of Mary is to enter, in mind and in heart, into the seven greatest expressions of Mary's co-suffering with the Redeemer of the world. Jesus' words to St. Bridget of Sweden convey this truth: "My Mother and I saved man as if with one Heart only: I by the suffering in my heart and my flesh; she by the sorrow and love of her heart."[1]

The mother in the book of Maccabees lost seven sons because of her unwavering fidelity to the Old Covenant (see 2 Macc. 7). The Mother of Christ experienced seven swords piercing her Immaculate Heart because of her unwavering fidelity to her Son in the New and everlasting Covenant. These seven experiences of sacrificial love with Jesus instruct every Christian on how to remain loyal to our Savior during life's greatest sufferings.

We rightly meditate upon Our Lady's Seven Sorrows to learn how to suffer well. Suffering is redemptive, for every suffering united to the infinite sufferings of Jesus becomes salvific, and no one embodies this better than the Immaculate Co-Redemptrix.

St. Alphonsus Liguori captures the supernatural sublimity of Christ's suffering and Mary's co-suffering like few others in

[1] *Revelations of St. Bridget* 9, 3.

the history of the Church. Joseph Hollcraft and Ruth Berghorst deserve the highest praise for directing the minds and hearts of twenty-first-century Christians back to the wisdom of this spiritually towering Doctor of the Church, that we might appreciate the fruits of his mystical meditations on the sorrows of the Blessed Mother, which necessarily redound to the infinitely meritorious sufferings of her Son, and for relating these sorrows to our present challenging moment of human history, in which suffering is ubiquitous. Hence, the clear imperative for this book.

May the readers of this book, through the contemplative fruits of its authors, find new or renewed appreciation for that Sorrowful and Immaculate Heart from whom we learn how best to suffer with Jesus, so that they can best share in His resounding victory, in which all sorrow turns into eternal joy.

—Dr. Mark Miravalle

PREFACE

Why another book on the Chaplet of the Seven Sorrows of Mary? Without dismissing the value of the beautiful books and booklets on this topic, we believe it is essential to consider this chaplet with a contemporary application—that is, considering Mary's sorrows in light of the sins of the twenty-first century that grieve the hearts of Jesus and Mary.

The Chaplet of the Seven Sorrows is a devotion that adds to our understanding of and love for our Blessed Mother. In praying this chaplet, we bring consolation to the heart of Our Lady and open our hearts to share in the salvific mission of bringing souls closer to the heart of Jesus Christ (see Col. 1:24). Intercessory prayer is that powerful (see James 5:16). God does not need our prayers in order to act. Still, He chooses to use our prayers in order to act. We do not change God's mind when we pray, but we bring to fruition what is in God's mind and heart. And we can be sure that holiness for every soul is in His mind and heart! Over the past two centuries, in private revelation, Mary has repeatedly expressed her sorrow over the sin in the world and how our sin wounds her heart and the heart of her Son. We need to start taking stock of our sins and to be ever aware of how we can help save souls for

Jesus Christ. The Chaplet of the Seven Sorrows of Mary is a tool to help us to do just that!

The Seven Sorrows Chaplet is not a replacement for the Rosary but, rather, a devotion directed to better understanding Mary's sorrowful journey and to pondering what each Marian suffering teaches us about our relationship with God and with one another. The more time we spend with Mary, the more insight we receive into our griefs and sorrows and the sadness and dejection around us. By praying the Seven Sorrows Chaplet, we enter Mary's classroom and learn to understand what is often interpreted as senseless.

A classroom devoted to Our Blessed Mother presupposes "books." One of the most profitable books we could read would be one about Our Lady's Seven Sorrows, showing us how to triumph over our temptations and trials, as she did. Among myriads of others she suffered, these Seven Sorrows were Satan's attempts to negate her vital contribution to our salvation, yet many people know little about those sorrows. This book seeks to familiarize Christians with the "book" of Our Lady's sorrows and the benefits our Lady has tied to this devotion.

ACKNOWLEDGMENTS

I want to first thank Dr. Mark Miravalle for his generous forward and timely advice in this project. Also, thanks to Bob Sutton for the gift of his time and editorial guidance. His constructive feedback was invaluable to the maturation of this work.

I extend a sincere thanks to the team at Sophia Institute Press, for their involvement in bringing this book to a conclusion, especially Nora Malone.

I would also like to offer a warm thank you to Ruth Berghorst, who not only co-authored this book but also provided the prayer support that propelled this writing project forward.

Most of all, I want to express my profound gratitude to my incredible wife, Jackie, for her countless sacrifices and loving way. I love you!

—Joseph Hollcraft
May 2, 2024
Feast of St. Athanasius

My profound gratitude and thanksgiving to Dr. Joseph Hollcraft, whose response to my initial inspiration for this book was a generous and enthusiastic yes! His admirable dedication to the spiritual formation of both priests and laity continues to challenge and inspire me.

For my husband, Glenn's, steadfast love, support, and encouragement, which enables and enhances everything in my life, I am truly grateful.

An initial friendship with my neighbor, Sarah Hondorp, became much more—transforming into the vehicle for my conversion to the Catholic Faith. Her subtle approach to evangelization enriched my life beyond measure and opened the door to a Marian devotion.

With humble gratitude, I acknowledge a trinity of servants of Christ in Carla Niziolek, Father Michael Burt, and the Women of the Word study group at Our Lady of the Lake Catholic Church in Holland, Michigan, for encouraging me and helping me to come home to the Faith.

Ad Jesum per Mariam.

—Ruth Berghorst
May 2, 2024
Feast of St. Athanasius

INTRODUCTION

Every Doctor of the Church is a saint, but not every saint is a Doctor of the Church. As of this writing, there are more than eleven thousand canonized saints but only thirty-seven Doctors of the Church. St. Alphonsus Liguori, the eighteenth-century bishop of Naples, is one of the thirty-seven. Why? His writings in moral theology helped steer souls away from the heresy of Jansenism (the imbalanced practice of rigor and asceticism in the spiritual life); his contributions to dogmatic theology and to apologetics are foundational to Catholic doctrine; and his ascetical and devotional writings, which have gone through several thousand editions and have been translated into more than fifty languages, have deepened the conversation on the interior life. While St. Teresa of Ávila, St. John of the Cross, and St. Thérèse of Lisieux are recognized as Doctors of the interior life, the broad-shouldered bishop St. Alphonsus is no less a master of the spiritual life.

His books on the spiritual life include *Prayer: The Great Means of Salvation and Perfection* and *The Glories of Mary*, in which St. Alphonsus invites us to pray with the Seven Sorrows of Mary as revealed in Sacred Scripture. As we seek to unite our hearts in contemplative prayer with the sorrowful heart of Mary, let us profit from the wisdom of St. Alphonsus Liguori both on prayer and on Mary, whom he referred to as the "Mother of the Miserable."

The initial inspiration for this work came from reading *The Contemplative Rosary with St. John Paul II and St. Teresa of Avila*, by Dan Burke and Connie Rossini. In that book is a clear catechesis on contemplation and how we ought to pray, as prescribed by St. Teresa of Avila and St. John Paul II. Similarly, the book you have in your hands will center on praying the Chaplet of the Seven Sorrows of Mary with a contemplative heart, guided by St. Alphonsus Liguori.

We hope that as you read these pages, the Holy Spirit will captivate your imagination and draw you into a deeper encounter with the Word of God, the sorrowful heart of Mary, and, most importantly, the Person of Jesus Christ. Ideally, the natural outgrowth of this encounter will yield a greater conviction to pray in reparation for the many sorrows that afflict the Church and, consequently, the hearts of Jesus and Mary.

First, we will examine the history of the Chaplet of the Seven Sorrows to help us understand why we pray it: to ponder more deeply our Lady's sorrowful heart and thereby dispose our hearts to be more generous in our spiritual almsgiving. Next, we will expound on mental prayer (meditation and contemplation) with St. Alphonsus Liguori so that we may properly meditate upon the Seven Sorrows of Mary. As St. Alphonsus writes, "Without mental prayer, the soul is without light."[2] Jesus asks us to share in His mercy and love in redemptive suffering, and we *can* do that well *only* if we adequately meditate upon the mystery of suffering. Meditating upon the sufferings of Jesus and Mary is light itself.

[2] St. Alphonsus Liguori, *Prayer: The Great Means of Salvation and Perfection* (Manchester, NH: Sophia Institute Press, 2021), 129.

Then, as Mary promises seven benefits to those who pray the chaplet—signal graces we are guaranteed to receive if we pray from the heart and are faithful to the teachings of the Church—we will take stock of the importance of a "promise" from Heaven.

Next, we will discuss how to pray the chaplet best; we will walk through the prayers that the chaplet comprises and explain the method of the contemplative chaplet. At the locus of this method of prayer will be reflections, probing questions, and intercessions that we hope will pull you into the biblical narrative that reveals the heartache of Mary.

Each Marian sorrow will be paired with a contemporary sorrow that, by our humble estimation, is worth praying in reparation for as part of our specific intercession. There are sorrows we must learn to grieve, and the Virgin Mary can help us to discern them. Jesus said, "Blessed are those who mourn, for they shall be comforted" (Matt. 5:4). Mary is the perfect disciple who grieves man's earthly plight. As we console her by our presence, she will teach us how to mourn. Mary, who is an icon of the Church, can help us to weep with her as our souls are pierced by the sword that pierces hers. The sorrows we will consider are more global, but we should not let that diminish the gravity of individual sin. The global topics under consideration are the outgrowth of individual sin. Every sin breaks the heart of the Mother, and this should humble us as we pray for the conversion of our hearts and our families and for the lifting of the shadow that is cast over the world in the seven contemporary sorrows.

Each contemporary sorrow will also be tied to the patron saint of that sorrow (or a relevant saint). For example, over the past decade, we have witnessed a rapid decline in mental health. To enrich our meditation and intercession, we will offer an account of this decline and turn for strength to St. Dymphna, the patron saint of those who struggle with mental health issues. Every saint in the Catholic Church has a God-given power to share in the dispensation of grace (see Rev. 5:8; 8:3–5); bringing select saints into the chaplet will supplement our musing on the Seven Sorrows.

Finally, in the appendix, we will pair each sorrow with one of the seven sacraments—this will enrich our sacramental sensibilities as we pray the Chaplet of the Seven Sorrows of Mary.

1

THE HISTORY OF THE CHAPLET

A Word on the Word of God

"And Simeon blessed them and said to Mary his mother, 'Behold, this child is set for the fall and rising of many in Israel, and for a sign that is spoken against (and a sword will pierce through your own soul also), that thoughts out of many hearts may be revealed' " (Luke 2:34–35). In this great Lucan passage, we have the foundation of the devotion to the Seven Sorrows of Mary, for what took place at the temple after Mary's Presentation of Jesus set in motion the spiritual practice of contemplating Mary's sorrows.

Seven Holy Men and St. Bridget of Sweden

While there are traces of religious devotion to Our Lady of Sorrows throughout the first millennium of the Church,[3] it was not until seven holy men of noble birth left the city of Florence, Italy, to seek solitude on Monte Senario that a more robust devotion to Mary would begin. These seven men, who sought to form a community devoted to prayer and penance, also had a particular

[3] Among other sources, we find in the fourth-century writings of St. Ambrose (a Doctor of the Church) and Ephrem the Syrian that Mary's sorrow was celebrated and venerated.

devotion to Our Lady. On Good Friday in 1239, while these men meditated on Our Lord's Passion and Mary's sufferings, Our Lady appeared to them. She revealed her wish for them to form an order dedicated to practicing and promoting devotion to her sorrows. In *The Glories of Mary*, St. Alphonsus Liguori writes, "With a black garment in her hand, she told them that if they wish to please her, they should often meditate upon her dolors [sorrows]."[4]

In response to Mary's request, the seven holy men began the religious order the Servants of Mary (or the Servites).[5] At the center of their devotional practice was the "Servite Rosary," also known today as the Chaplet of the Seven Sorrows of Mary—the devotional practice of meditating on Mary's passion. The devotion quickly spread throughout Italy and beyond.[6]

As the Chaplet of the Seven Sorrows became a regular devotion in the life of the Church, it received a new gust of wind in the visions of St. Bridget of Sweden (1303–1373). At age ten, Bridget experienced her first mystical vision, informing her of the number of blows Jesus received during His Passion (5,480 blows). From then on, she had a particular devotion to the Passion of Christ. Bridget would experience regular visions of Jesus, Mary, and the angels, often focusing on the sorrowful hearts of Jesus and Mary.

In one vision, Our Lady pleaded with St. Bridget:

4 St. Alphonsus Maria de Liguori, *The Glories of Mary* (Charlotte, NC: TAN Books, 1968), 393.

5 These men, Buonfiglio Monaldo, Alexis Falconieri, Benedict dell' Antella, Bartholomew Amidei, Ricovero Uguccione, Gerardino Sostegni, and John Buonagiunta, were canonized in 1888. Alban Butler, "The Seven Holy Founders of the Servite Order," EWTN, https://www.ewtn.com/catholicism/library/seven-holy-founders-of-the-servite-order-5160.

6 Ann Ball, *Encyclopedia of Catholic Devotions and Practices* (Huntington, IN: Our Sunday Visitor, 2003), 487.

> I look around at everyone in the world to see if there happens to be some who might have compassion on me and be mindful of my sorrow, but I find very few who think about my sorrow and tribulation. This is why, my daughter, although I am forgotten and neglected by many people, you must not forget me! Look at my struggles and imitate them as far as you can! *Contemplate my sorrows and tears and be sorry that the friends of God are so few. Stand* firm! Look, my Son is coming.[7]

Alongside this appeal to contemplate the dolors of Mary, Our Lady also promised signal graces to those who practiced devotion to her Seven Sorrows (we will explore these in a separate chapter). Undoubtedly, these promises factor greatly in the rise of the devotion to Our Lady of Sorrows.

Our Lady of Sorrows and Fátima

As this devotion increased among the faithful, and as a response to the Protestant Hussites (the group that left sword marks on the face of the image of Our Lady of Czestochowa),[8] the provincial synod

[7] *The Revelations of St. Bridget of Sweden: Books 1–5*, ed. Darrell Wright (self-pub., CreateSpace Independent Publishing, 2016), bk. 2, chap. 24, emphasis added.

[8] In 1430, the Hussites, followers of the heretical priest John Hus, attacked a monastery of the Pauline Fathers, caretakers of the image of Our Lady of Czestochowa, and plundered the sanctuary. They stole the image and put it in their wagon but found that their horses, after a few steps, would not pull the wagon any farther. The Hussites threw the image on the ground, and one of them drew his sword and slashed the image twice, causing two deep gashes on the cheek of the Blessed Virgin; while attempting to slash the image again, he was overcome by an agony and died.

of Cologne instituted the feast of Our Lady of Sorrows in 1413. In 1482, the feast was added to the missal under the title "Our Lady of Compassion." In 1817, Pope Pius VII, while in captivity during the Napoleonic wars, found consolation by praying to Our Lady of Sorrows and composed a litany to her (see the appendix), and once he was liberated, he extended the feast of Our Lady of Compassion to the universal Church. In 1913, Pope St. Pius X placed the feast on September 15 so that it would be close to the feast of the Holy Cross, on September 14.[9] He renamed the feast day "Our Lady of Sorrows" to focus on Mary's intense suffering during Christ's Passion and death.[10]

This action by the Holy Father was confirmed by Heaven only a few years later when, on October 13, 1917, during her last apparition at Fátima and after the Miracle of the Sun, Mary appeared not only as Our Lady of the Rosary and Our Lady of Mount Carmel but also as *Our Lady of Sorrows.*

Mary's emphasis at Fátima on prayer, repentance, conversion, and reparation for sins fits in seamlessly with the visions of St. Bridget of Sweden. Also, her appearance as Our Lady of Sorrows reminds us of her grieving heart over the sins of her children and the need for us to console her pierced heart.[11]

Despite attempts to repair the image, these two slashes and one from an earlier attack have always reappeared.

9 St. Alphonsus Liguori was beatified on September 15, 1816. Evidently, the Holy Spirit sees fit that we see the beautiful relationship between St. Alphonsus Liguori and Our Lady of Sorrows.

10 Fr. Paul Haffner, "Our Lady of Sorrows," *Inside the Vatican*, September 2004.

11 Concurrent with the historical snapshot of Our Lady of Sorrows, St. Alphonsus documents the many saints who have honored and venerated Mary's grief. These include St. Bernadine, who exclaimed: "If all the sorrows of the world were united, they would

Our Lady of Kibeho

On March 2, 1982, Mary appeared to Marie Claire Mukangango in Kibeho, Rwanda, and said, "One must meditate on the Passion of Jesus, and on the deep sorrows of His Mother. One must recite the Rosary every day, and also the Rosary of the Seven Sorrows of Mary, to obtain the favor of repentance."[12] Marie Claire reported witnessing the Virgin Mary in tears on August 15, 1982. The sorrow of the Mother of God stemmed from the disbelief and absence of repentance among people. The tears of Mary were a sacrament of the profound grief of her wounded heart.

Marie Claire followed the command to spread devotion to Mary's sorrowful heart but died only twelve years later (in 1994) during civil unrest. Immaculée Ilibagiza, the Rwandan woman who was famously "left to tell" of Mary's message, has continued the work of Marie Claire.[13] She has traveled the world echoing

---

not equal that of the glorious Virgin Mary." And St. Bonaventure added, "Our Lady, where art thou? Near the Cross? No, rather, thou art on the Cross, crucified, sacrificing thyself with thy Son." See Liguori, *The Glories of Mary*, 395.

[12] Immaculée Ilibaziga, *Our Lady of Kibeho: Mary Speaks to the World from the Heart of Africa* (Carlsbad, CA: Hay House, 2010), 185. On June 29, 2001, Augustin Misago, bishop of Gikongoro, released the final judgment, which was also approved by the Holy See, that Our Lady did appear at Kibeho to Alphonsine Mumureke (age seventeen), Nathalie Mukamazimpaka (age twenty), and Marie Clare Mukangango (age twenty-one).

[13] *Left to Tell* is a poignant memoir by Immaculée Ilibagiza, who lived through the Rwandan genocide. The title *Left to Tell* carries profound meaning in her narrative. As a Tutsi woman in Rwanda during the 1994 genocide, Immaculée experienced the intense conflict between the Hutu and Tutsi ethnic groups, which led to a devastating massacre. Despite the traumatic violence and the loss of her family, Immaculée's life was spared. For ninety-one days,

the message of Our Lady of Kibeho with the same conviction and fervor as Marie Claire. In her book, *Our Lady of Kibeho,* Immaculée summarized:

> During her visitations to Kibeho, the Holy Virgin revealed that this rosary possesses immense spiritual power for those who say it sincerely. She promised that when prayed with an open and repentant heart, the rosary would win the Lord's forgiveness for our sins and free our souls from guilt and remorse. She also promised that over time, the rosary would develop within us a deeper understanding of *why* we sin, and that knowledge would give us the wisdom and strength to change or remove any internal flaws or weaknesses of character causing unhappiness and keeping us from enjoying the joyous life God intended for us to live.[14]

We have witnessed a modern revival of the Servite Rosary with Mary's appearance in Kibeho. It is now up to us to respond to this call to pray the Chaplet of the Seven Sorrows. Mary's message to the Rwandans more than forty years ago ought to resonate with us:

> The world is rebellious against God; it commits too many sins; it has neither love nor peace.... If you do not repent and do not convert your hearts, you will fall into the abyss. The world is evil and rushes towards its ruin. It is about to fall into its abyss. The world is in rebellion against God.

---

she concealed herself in a cramped bathroom, fervently praying. The phrase "left to tell" signifies her miraculous survival—she remained when countless others did not. Immaculée views her survival as purposeful; she wasn't just preserved; she was destined to share the account of those harrowing times.

[14] Ilibaziga, *Our Lady of Kibeho*, 187.

> Many sins are being committed. There is no love and no peace. If you do not repent and convert your hearts, you will all fall into an abyss.[15]

As we step back to consider the importance of Mary's message and the urgent call to respond to Mary with a heart full of love, let us be mindful that exploring the history of the chaplet is more than just recounting a series of chronological events: it is envisioning our prayerful response as a free act that steers the course of history.

15 "Elements of the Message of Kibeho," Kibeho Sanctuary, http://www.kibeho-sanctuary.com/en/apparitions/message.html.

2

WHY THE CHAPLET?

Into Thy Word

Why should we pray the Chaplet of the Seven Sorrows of Mary? First, we pray the chaplet because it involves praying Scripture, which deepens our relationship with God. God's Word meets all our needs, "profitable for teaching, for reproof, for correction, and for training in righteousness, that the man of God may be complete, equipped for every good work" (2 Tim. 3:16–17). Engaging with the Word of God not only educates us but also transforms our hearts and lives. St. Jerome's words should echo in our hearts: "Ignorance of Scripture is ignorance of Christ." To this, we might add that ignorance of Scripture is ignorance of Mary as well. Pontius Pilate's declaration "Ecce homo" ("Behold the man") in referring to Christ (see John 19:5), is what we do when we study Scripture. Similarly, when we reflect on the Seven Sorrows of Mary in Scripture, we "ecce mulieris" (behold the woman). To pray the Chaplet of Seven Sorrows is to sink deeper into the Word of God!

Why Practice a Devotion?

Second, as we embark on the question of why we should pray the devotional of the Chaplet of the Seven Sorrows, we should first take up the topic of *devotions* in the life of the Church.

Devotions are popular prayers and pious practices through which we worship God or venerate Mary and the saints. For more than two thousand years, the faithful have used these various practices to infuse their everyday lives with prayer; in fact, they help us to follow St. Paul's admonition to pray without ceasing (1 Thess. 5:17). Examples include novenas, processions, adoration of the Blessed Sacrament, the Rosary, the Stations of the Cross, the veneration of relics, and chaplets, such as the Chaplet of the Seven Sorrows of Mary. Often, devotions express a particular conviction about the object of the devotion: adoration of the Blessed Sacrament expresses the conviction about the True Presence of Jesus Christ in the Blessed Sacrament; praying the Rosary expresses the belief in Mary's role in the dispensation of grace; devotion to saints expresses confidence in their roles as spiritual companions, guides, and mediators.[16]

Properly used, popular devotional practices never replace liturgical life but complement it and extend it into daily life. Any devotion, including the sacrifices required for its practice, ought to deepen a person's "amen" to Christ in the Eucharist.

The faithful practice of popular devotions can help us experience God in our everyday lives and conform us more closely to Jesus Christ—enriching our spiritual lives.

Why Pray to Mary?

Marian devotion is the practice of honoring and venerating the Mother of Jesus through prayer and reflection. Honoring Mary has been an integral part of Catholic devotion for centuries. But why?

[16] Congregation for Divine Worship and the Discipline of the Sacraments, *Directory on Popular Piety and the Liturgy, Principles and Guidelines*, no. 8.

God chose Mary, and her intercession mediates divinity, as exemplified in the Wedding Feast at Cana (see John 2:1–12). St. Alphonsus believed that since God gave us Jesus through Mary, the surest way for us to go to Jesus is through Mary.[17] St. Alphonsus's confidence in Mary's intercession is rooted in Sacred Scripture and the Deposit of Faith. It is clear that Mary's yes at the Annunciation enabled the human presence of God in the world (see Luke 1:26–38). And, as John records, the first miracle performed by Jesus was due to the direct mediation of Mary (see John 2:1–12). If we desire to do the same—to make Jesus uniquely present and to prompt His action through our intercessory prayer—we ought to place our petitions into the immaculate hands of Mary and allow her to turn them over to her Son.

We pray to Mary because Jesus has given us His Blessed Mother as *our* great spiritual Mother. On the Cross, Jesus, even amidst the anguish of body and mind He was enduring, looked down upon the beloved disciple John and said to Mary, "Behold, your son," and to the beloved disciple, "Behold, your mother" (John 19:26–27). St. Alphonsus states that when our Lord said, "Behold, your son" to Mary, it amounted to "Behold, the whole human race, which right now is being born to the life of grace because you are offering My life for the salvation of all."[18] John is the beloved disciple, but throughout the Gospel, he is portrayed as the icon of every disciple whom Jesus loves. Just as all baptized believers have God as their Father and Jesus as an elder Brother, they have Mary as their spiritual Mother.[19] "Jesus was Mary's first-born in the flesh, but all humankind was second-born according to the spirit."[20]

[17] Liguori, *The Glories of Mary*, 126.
[18] Liguori, *The Glories of Mary*, 29.
[19] See the *Catechism of the Catholic Church* (CCC), no. 501.
[20] Liguori, *The Glories of Mary*, 27.

On the Cross, Jesus was in anguish, and so was Mary. As we will discuss in greater detail in our meditation of the first sorrow, Simeon's prophecy that a sword would pierce the heart of Mary is a kind of second annunciation. In the words of Pope St. John Paul II:

> Simeon's words (of a sorrowful sword) seem like a second Annunciation to Mary, for they tell her of the actual historical situation in which the Son is to accomplish his mission, namely, in misunderstanding and sorrow.... It reveals to Mary that she will have to live her obedience of faith in suffering, at the side of the suffering Savior, and that her motherhood will be mysterious and sorrowful.[21]

St. Alphonsus says that Mary's pain exceeded all the pains a human heart could endure.[22] This is important because it was in this historical moment of unprecedented agony suffered by Jesus and His Mother that Jesus entrusted to Mary's care the disciple whom He loved. It is as if He looks into the heart of every faithful disciple He loves and says: "You will endure unspeakable trial, but I am now giving you a gift, my Mother, in this incomprehensible moment of suffering, to give you consolation and hope. She will be in solidarity with you every step of the way." For this reason, we should never hesitate to fly to Mary to obtain all the graces we need to walk confidently in God's love and to be people of holy perseverance.

People often ask, "Why pray to Mary when we can go directly to Jesus?" The simple answer might be another question: "Why

[21] Pope John Paul II, encyclical letter on the Mother of God *Redemptoris Mater* (March 25, 1987), no. 16.

[22] St. Alphonsus Maria de Liguori, *The Passion and the Death of Jesus Christ*, 2nd edition (Philadelphia: Aeterna Press, 2015), 212.

do we ask others to pray for us when we need intercessory prayer?" When we require prayer, we turn to those we believe are close to Jesus—those Christians who are prayerful and in tune with the Holy Spirit. If you are on a gurney, you want trained doctors who are concerned about bringing you back to health to attend to you. There is no one closer to Jesus and no one more concerned about your spiritual health than Mary. Like any mother, Mary is concerned about the brokenness of her children. And more than any mother, she understands the brokenness of your heart. Take to heart the wisdom of St. Anselm: "The dignity of the intercessor may supply for our poverty."[23]

St. Paul assures us that God is gracious in His favor to answer many prayers (see 2 Cor. 1:11). If the fervent prayer of the righteous person has great power (see James 5:16–18), then how much more can the intercessory prayers of the Mother of God affect the salvation of your soul and bring light to the dark corners of your heart?

Speaking of light, St. Alphonsus reminds us that it is by the two great lights of creation that we can further appreciate why we pray to Mary:

> In the first chapter of the Book of Genesis we read that *God made two great lights; a greater light to rule the day; and a lesser light to rule the night* (Gen. 1:16). Cardinal Hugo says that "Christ is the greater light to rule the just, and Mary the lesser to rule the sinners"; meaning that the sun is a figure of Jesus Christ, whose light is enjoyed by the just who live in the clear day of divine grace; and that the moon is a figure of Mary, by whose means those who are in the

[23] Quoted in Liguori, *Prayer*, 27–28.

night of sin are enlightened. Since Mary is this auspicious luminary, and is so for the benefit of poor sinners, should anyone have been so unfortunate as to fall into the night of sin, what is he to do? Innocent III replies, "Whoever is in the night of sin, let him cast his eyes on the moon, let him implore Mary" (*In Assumpt.* s. 2). Since he has lost the light of the sun of justice by losing the grace of God, let him turn to the moon, and beseech Mary. She will certainly give him light to see the misery of his state, and strength to leave it without delay. St. Methodius says "that by the prayers of Mary almost innumerable sinners are converted" (*Paciucch. in Ps.* lxxxvi. *exc.* 17).[24]

Just as the moon's light reflects the sun without diminishing it, so does Mary reflect the light of Christ without reducing it. With the moon under her feet (see Rev. 12:1), Mary crushes the head of the serpent (see Gen. 3:15) and draws us into her Son's light—exposing the serpent's dark ways. The mere invocation of the name of Mary sends the serpent running: "The devils not only fear but tremble at the very sound of her sacred name. As men fall prostrate with fear if a thunderbolt falls near them, so do the demons if they hear the name of Mary. The evil spirits greatly fear the Queen of Heaven, and flee at the sound of her name, as if from fire. At the very sound of the word Mary, they are cast down as if by thunder."[25] Before we go any further, we should pause and put the name of Mary on our lips. In fact, entering the school of Marian prayer should always start with the holy names of Jesus and Mary in our hearts and on our lips.

[24] Liguori, *The Glories of Mary*, 93.

[25] Liguori, *The Glories of Mary*, 118.

The Marian school of prayer is one of light and exposure—the exposure that occurs when something is revealed. We pray to Mary not only for specific petitions but also to learn how to pray better.

How does Mary teach us to pray better? In the Gospel of Luke, we read, "And [the shepherds] went with haste, and found Mary and Joseph, and the babe lying in a manger. And when they saw it they made known the saying which had been told them concerning this child; and all who heard it wondered at what the shepherds told them. But Mary kept all these things, pondering them in her heart" (Luke 2:16–19). After this narrative, some thirty verses later, Luke records the episode of Mary's finding Jesus in the Temple after having lost Him for three days. Upon finding Jesus in the Temple, Luke writes, "And he said to them, 'How is it that you sought me? Did you not know that I must be in my Father's house?' And they did not understand the saying which he spoke to them. And he went down with them and came to Nazareth and was obedient to them; and his mother kept all these things in her heart" (Luke 2:49–51).

In each narrative, we read of Mary's thinking carefully about the mysterious events that were unfolding before her. In its English rendering, the word employed for "thinking carefully" is *pondering*. What are we to make of this word? The Greek word for "pondering," *symballein*, also means "to throw together," "to compare and weigh facts," or "to piece together." In effect, Mary was balancing and counterbalancing the revelation that she was the Mother of God. She weighed and measured the wider meaning of losing God for three days to find Him discoursing with the teachers preaching in the Temple. Mary had a lot to "think carefully" about: she had had no sexual relations, yet she had a baby, and her twelve-year-old Son left the family caravan to listen and teach in the Temple. What we see in Mary's pondering is not only a weighing but also a piecing together of a series of events that she was slowly coming to understand.

Something to remember here is the principle of divine grace beautifully seen in the life of Mary. As Peter Kreeft notes:

> Supernatural grace does not bypass human nature, or substitute for it. Grace turns nature on, not off. And especially human nature. And since human free will is an essential dimension of human nature, divine grace turns our human free will and free choice on, not off. The more grace, the more nature. The more grace, the more freedom. The more God, the more us. It's like the relation between light and colors: the more light there is, the more each color shines.[26]

Mary was not God's robot. "Full of grace," she maintained her free will. She could have said no to God's plan, like Eve, the first mother of the living, but she did not. Mary's free yes to God brings light and insight into the depths of her sacrifices, sorrows, and sufferings. All of the myriad yeses throughout her life were offered in complete cooperation with the Holy Spirit. With every yes, Mary was freer to cooperate with God's mission and bring to fruition God's plan for her here on Earth—and that cooperation continues.

When we ponder with Mary, we learn how to ponder fluently, which is a necessary step in defeating the enemy.

As mentioned earlier, the Greek term translated as "ponder," *symballein*, meaning "to throw together," is in direct contrast with the Greek *diaballein*, which means "to throw across; to scatter." From *diaballein* we get the English word *diabolical*, which we often translate as "belonging to Satan." Satan's function is to leave us

[26] Peter Kreeft, *Food for the Soul: Reflections on the Mass Readings, Cycle C* (Washington, DC: Word on Fire Institute, 2021), 13.

"scattered"—thrown asunder, confused about everyday life. We overcome the Tempter's tactics by "piecing together"—that is, by making sense of, through God's grace, what God wants us to make sense of. We overcome Satan's *diaballein* by imitating Mary's *symballein*. Indeed, there is enmity between Mary and Satan (see Gen. 3:15) as she teaches us how to pray better and follow her example of intercessory prayer.[27]

As we consider why we ought to pray the Chaplet of the Seven Sorrows by reflecting upon why we ought to pray to Mary, it is worthwhile to examine the topic of intercessory prayer in more depth. After all, praying for the living and the dead is a spiritual work of mercy, and so is comforting the sorrowful and the afflicted—another reason we pray the chaplet.

A Work of Mercy

Mercy is usually equated with its physical or corporal dimension: feeding the hungry, giving drink to the thirsty, sheltering the homeless, and so on. Rarely—at least in our experience—do we equate mercy with the spiritual work of comforting the sorrowful and the afflicted.[28]

This spiritual work of mercy has a direct connection to the sorrowful heart of Mary: to comfort the *sorrowful* and the afflicted.

[27] For a similar discussion on the role of Mary in our intercessory prayer, see Joseph Hollcraft, *Unleashing the Power of Intercessory Prayer* (Manchester, NH: Sophia Institute Press, 2020), 144.

[28] The traditional corporal works of mercy are as follows: to feed the hungry, to give drink to the thirsty, to clothe the naked, to shelter the homeless, to visit the sick, to visit the imprisoned, and to bury the dead. The traditional spiritual works of mercy are these: to instruct the ignorant, to counsel the doubtful, to admonish sinners, to bear wrongs patiently, to forgive offenses willingly, to comfort the afflicted, and to pray for the living and the dead.

In our day, people have attempted to remove suffering through abortion, euthanasia, and suicide. Sometimes we are under the impression that we can undo suffering, but often the very attempt to undo suffering is the cause of more suffering, which we sweep under the rug. Christ did not come to undo suffering but to give it meaning—to help us understand suffering and to give it redemptive value. While on Earth, Christ taught us how to comfort the sorrowful, the burdened, and those experiencing deep sadness.

Throughout the Gospels, we see Jesus comforting the sorrowful. He was moved with pity for the widow of Nain (Luke 7:13). When the daughter of Jairus died, Jesus went to the home of her parents, who were weeping and mourning (Luke 8:51). Jesus went to Bethany to be with Martha and Mary after their brother died and wept with them (John 11:35). In fact, "Jesus wept" is the shortest verse in the Bible, yet it is packed with the most extraordinary depth—the depth of the heart that feels our aches. The tears of Jesus are a visible reminder of the Father's compassion for man's grief.[29] In the end, Jesus healed many, granted peace to countless

[29] Grief is a natural response to loss, whether it's the death of a loved one, a personal tragedy, or any form of suffering. Catholics recognize that sorrow is part of the human experience (human nature), and it's essential to acknowledge and process it. Grief can be good as it involves being honest about our feelings. Weeping signifies deep trust. Often, one can shed tears only in the presence of someone who provides a sense of safety and vulnerability. Offering our tears to God during times of suffering is not an indication of weak faith; rather, it is a testament to our faith, deepening it as we entrust our sorrows to Him, just as a child would trust in a parent. Ultimately, experiencing sorrow in response to suffering is natural and acceptable. Moreover, it can be a path to sanctity when one entrusts this sorrow to God, as Mary exemplified.

people, and even guaranteed Paradise to one (see Luke 23:43). His was a ministry of comforting the sorrowful and the afflicted—a ministry of presence.

We share in the merciful work of Jesus in the world by invoking the presence of the Holy Spirit, who is the Comforter (see Acts 9:31) and who brings the divine gifts of consolation and peace.

How do we practice this spiritual work of mercy, to comfort the sorrowful and the afflicted? First, be aware that the ministry of presence does not always require a voice. In fact, often it calls for silence. A respectful silence can be a way of honoring grief and signaling true camaraderie. St. Paul says, "Weep with those who weep" (Rom. 12:15), and so we do. The God-Man's weeping is quietly powerful. So we rely on Mary's guidance and ask her how to proceed.

The Chaplet of the Seven Sorrows is a particular gift because a good meditation on the Seven Sorrows of Mary will bring insight into how to be in solidarity with the suffering. Through the chaplet, we learn not from just any teacher but from the queen of teachers herself. We should let her lead: she may inspire us to cook a meal, to send a card, or to have a Mass said. We must adhere to her promptings to be present to a grieving person.

What's more, as you pray with Mary, be open to going to the soul who is distressed and grieving. Again, presence is important. As the promptings of the Holy Spirit lead you, pray the Chaplet of the Seven Sorrows with the distressed soul. If you are physically distant from the afflicted person, pray with him or her over the phone. If neither is possible, invite the presence of the Holy Spirit into your prayer, and ask the Holy Spirit to make His presence known to the one you are praying for. God the Father would like nothing more than to lavish His grace and deep consolation upon a soul who is in need.

As you pray the Chaplet of the Seven Sorrows, Mary will teach you how to be the face, the love, and the voice, when needed, to comfort the sorrowful and the afflicted.

Up to this point, we have emphasized the importance of consoling those around us, but what about Mary herself? Mary is grieving, and our prayer brings her consolation. How? In our mind, we can bring solace to Mary's sorrowful heart in three ways.

First, by praying with Mary in meditating on the Seven Sorrows that pierced her heart: the entirety of this devotion is an accompaniment with Mary that brings her consolation. St. Alphonsus recounts the words of Mary to St. Bridget of Sweden: "I look around upon all who are in the world, if perchance there may be any to pity me, and meditate upon my sorrows."[30] Comprehending Mary's sorrow will take a lifetime. Comforting anyone who is grieving or in great sorrow requires extraordinary patience, sensitivity, and willingness to listen. God's tempo is often not our own. We encourage you to pray for patience to better understand Mary's grieving heart.

The other two ways in which we may console Mary's heart are best understood in terms of her title "Refuge of Sinners," under which she has been revered for more than a thousand years.

We ourselves are among the "sinners" who should find their refuge in Mary. The first words of the Gospel, "Repent, and believe in the gospel" (Mark 1:15), are for all of us. The evangelist reminds us, "If we say we have no sin, we deceive ourselves, and the truth is not in us" (1 John 1:8). Before we pray for the world's problems, we must pray for the conversion of our own hearts.

Praying with the grieving Mary will transform how we see ourselves, our loved ones, and humanity. It will steep our hearts in humility, give us a new perspective, and open our souls to unseen

[30] Liguori, *The Glories of Mary*, 395.

graces that are imperative in a time of increasing adversity. Praying with Our Lady of Sorrows will unveil which of our behaviors causes her pain and what steps we must take to remedy those behaviors. Praying to Our Lady of Sorrows can also reveal what we don't yet understand is causing us suffering. We might be tied to some demonic stronghold or a pattern of vice that we don't see. When we pray the Chaplet of the Seven Sorrows, we pray for contrite hearts—for sorrow for our offenses against the Immaculate Heart of Mary and the Sacred Heart of Jesus. In *The Glories of Mary*, St. Alphonsus speaks of a blessing that Our Lord will grant: "That those who invoked the divine mother by her sorrows before death will merit to obtain true repentance of all their sins."[31] Our consolation is Mary's consolation because it means the salvation of our souls.

The more we accompany Mary in meditating upon her sorrows and making our conversion a priority, the better we will be disposed to console her in the third way: by praying for unrepentant sinners. John's message is clear: "We know that God does not listen to sinners, but if any one is a worshiper of God and does his will, God listens to him" (John 9:31). St. Alphonsus notes, "When souls seek to love the Lord, He finds it impossible not to love them in return."[32] These words should humble us.

Praying the Chaplet of the Seven Sorrows with the intention of increasing repentance for our sins is good, but if there is no accompanying intention to pray for those who live in grave sin, then Mary's heart will be less consoled. In one of St. Bridget's visions, an angel spoke of Mary's great consolation: "It may be said that this was the only consolation of Mary in the midst of her great

[31] Liguori, *The Glories of Mary*, 402.

[32] St. Alphonsus Liguori, *Alphonsus Liguori: Selected Writings*, Classics of Western Spirituality Series (New York: Paulist Press, 1999), 97.

sorrow at the passion of her Son, to see the lost world redeemed by his death, and men, who were his enemies, reconciled with God."[33] Indeed, the angel's use of the word *only* suggests that the conversion of those headed for eternal destruction is Mary's greatest consolation. We can imagine why the angel would say such a thing when we consider Mary looking upon her Son, who experienced 5,480 blows; that every wound was necessary to open the door for even the most egregious sinner whose sin involves grave matter.[34]

Many of us pray the Chaplet of the Seven Sorrows of Mary for unrepentant souls. As illustrated in our treatment of intercessory prayer, our fervent prayer has efficacious power in saving souls and changing the course of history (see James 5:16).

Mary has asked us to offer prayers and reparations for the sins of the world, and we remove the swords from her heart when we do that. This brings us to our final topic in this chapter: redemptive suffering.

What Is the Value of Our Suffering?

What is redemptive suffering? In what is arguably one of the more misunderstood texts in all of Sacred Scripture, St. Paul writes, "Now I rejoice in my sufferings for your sake, and in my flesh, I complete what is lacking in Christ's afflictions for the sake of his body, that is, the church" (Col. 1:24). Pay close attention to St. Paul's words,

[33] Liguori, *The Glories of Mary*, 399.

[34] "*Grave matter* is specified by the Ten Commandments, corresponding to the answer of Jesus to the rich young man: 'Do not kill, Do not commit adultery, Do not steal, Do not bear false witness, Do not defraud, Honor your father and your mother.' The gravity of sins is more or less great: murder is graver than theft. One must also take into account who is wronged: violence against parents is in itself graver than violence against a stranger" (CCC 1858).

because they can be easily misinterpreted. What is lacking has nothing to do with Christ's sufferings; rather, it concerns the afflictions upon the entire Church, which St. Paul admits he has contributed to. What is lacking, then, is our cooperation with God in uniting our afflictions with the affliction of Christ's Passion for the salvation of souls. Christ's wounds, in a sense, have become a portal to enter more profoundly into the salvific, redemptive mission of the Church. Pope St. John Paul II writes that man cannot add anything to the sufferings of Christ, but "in the mystery of the Church as his Body, Christ has in a sense opened his own redemptive suffering to all human suffering."[35] This is good news! Again, Jesus does not remove suffering but gives it redemptive power. He wastes nothing. Man wastes a lot of things, including suffering. There is a lot of wasted suffering in the world when people fail to unite their sufferings to the Cross of Christ. We all experience pain, strife, illness, and mental and physical anguish, but the good news is that our suffering is not useless; it is the most useful thing in the redemptive mission of Christ. There is nothing quick about suffering, but in faith, it speeds up our need for God's grace to assist in saving souls. There is nothing else that cries out—"anything else"—more than suffering, and yet there is nothing else that draws us closer to the heart of Christ. Suffering is often the greatest inconvenience of our day, but love is defined by how we act in that inconvenience.

The words of St. Paul ought to be understood in relation to redemptive suffering's objective and subjective aspects. *Objective redemption* is the historical work of the Cross, the graces obtained by the merits of Jesus Christ for the forgiveness of sins, a once-and-for-all work. *Subjective redemption* is how those graces are released

[35] Pope John Paul II, apostolic letter on the Christian meaning of human suffering *Salvifici Doloris* (February 11, 1984), no. 29.

upon every person in every generation. When we unite our suffering with Christ's suffering, we do not obtain graces for the soul we are praying for—that has already been accomplished—but we help release the graces already merited by Jesus Christ. Jesus is so good to us; He says: "You desire to see your loved ones in Heaven. Help me release the graces I have already won on the Cross by suffering for them. Help me to help your loved ones!" You might say to Jesus, "This is too hard." Jesus would agree with you. He would say, "Exactly. It is humanly impossible; that's why I sent the gift of the Holy Spirit to assist you. You got this because I got you!"

Two people might experience the same cross—say, the loss of a job or the death of a loved one—but may respond to it differently; the cross might lead one soul closer to God and the other further away from Him.[36] Why? Because they differ in their disposition. Some carry their crosses humbly and patiently, acknowledging that they deserve whatever cross Divine Providence has laid upon their backs; others curse their crosses and are bitter and angry at what is happening to them. Remember the two thieves crucified alongside Christ: the repentant thief enters Heaven by his cross; the unrepentant thief meets punishment through his cross. Our Lady knows the details of every cross and will always be there to assist us in carrying our crosses well (see the meditation on the Fourth Sorrow). Still, she cannot and will not twist our arms to get us to do something "against our will"; she will obtain the grace, and we must cooperate with the grace and use it as our Father desires.

We tend to shrink back in fear and disgust at the prospect of suffering. But as members of Christ's Body, we all must do what

[36] Victor Frankl details this in his work *Man's Search for Meaning* (Boston: Beacon Press, 2006), the extraordinary account of what he witnessed in the Auschwitz concentration camp.

He has done. Participating in God's work of salvation for men and ourselves is a great blessing. St. Alphonsus remarks, "Was Christ's Passion insufficient to save? Nothing was lacking in the value of his Passion; it was more than sufficient for the salvation of all men. And yet, to have the merits of Christ's Passion applied to us, we need to cooperate, patiently suffering the toils and tribulations God may wish to send us, to liken us more closely to his Son Jesus."[37] Liguori's words "to liken us more closely to his Son Jesus" are paramount. Essentially, he is saying that redemptive suffering transforms us more and more into Christ Himself. If we want to be Christlike, we must do what He did: suffer for the sake of souls.

For Catholics, then, the suffering that God allows us to experience is but a reality to be embraced and offered to God through Christ Jesus. In Baptism, we have been incorporated into the Mystical Body of Christ. This is an invitation to participate in the mystical outpouring of God's merciful love (see 2 Pet. 1:4). In offering up our sufferings redemptively for the conversion of souls, we are fulfilling our baptismal call as true members of Christ's Body.

The phrase "reparation for sins" was used in the opening chapter. Reparation is the "act of making amends for a wrong done or for an offense, especially for sin, which is an offense against God."[38] In the word *reparation*, we hear the word *repair* (the Latin word *reparatio is* translated as "repairing" or "restoring"). Acts of reparation repair your relationship with Jesus Christ. The penance you receive from a priest in Confession is an example of this kind of reparation.

Making reparation to God leads naturally to the work of Christian co-redemption. Pope St. John Paul II stated that all Christians

[37] Liguori, *The Passion and the Death of Jesus Christ*, 31.

[38] CCC, glossary, s.v. "reparation"; see also no. 2487.

are called to be co-redeemers with Christ. When our suffering is given to God to make amends for ourselves or others, this reparation restores man to God. In this sense, making reparation and redemptive suffering are interlinked.

Sharing in Christ's mission of co-redemption brings great consolation to the heart of Mary. Mary exemplified the ministry of co-redemption most gloriously with her fiat at the Annunciation, when God became man, and again at the foot of the Cross, where she suffered alongside her Son. When Christians bring Christ to others and spread the gospel, they participate in co-redemption.

In summary, when we work to make reparation to the Sacred Heart of Jesus and the Immaculate Heart of Mary, we work to satisfy God's justice on behalf of ourselves and our fellow men. In this, we are entering more deeply into the salvific work of Christ on the Cross as He worked to make the ultimate reparation on our behalf. He became the one Mediator between God and man (see 1 Tim. 2:5; Heb. 7:25). As His disciples, we have the privilege of entering into that mediation and participating in His priestly ministry on behalf of our brothers and sisters who do not yet know Him (see Col. 1:24; Phil. 4:6–7). We all suffer in this life. The question is: What will we do with that suffering? Will we invite Jesus into it? In his work *Divine Intimacy*, Fr. Gabriel of St. Mary Magdalen tells us that we are invited to contemplate Mary's sorrows, "sympathize with her, and ask for the invaluable grace of sharing with her in the Passion of Jesus." He goes on to say, "Let us remember that this participation is not to be merely sentimental, but must lead us to real *compassion*, that is, to *suffering with* Jesus and Mary. The sufferings God sends us have no other purpose."[39]

[39] Fr. Gabriel of St. Mary Magdalen, *Divine Intimacy* (London: Baronius Press, 2008), 375.

3

HOW DO WE PRAY WITH A CONTEMPLATIVE HEART?

Mental Prayer: Meditation and Contemplation

As we mentioned in the introduction, this book centers on praying the Chaplet of the Seven Sorrows with a contemplative heart. But what does it mean to pray with a contemplative heart?

Meditation and contemplation are two forms of mental prayer. In his work *Prayer: The Great Means of Salvation and Perfection*, St. Alphonsus says that mental prayer is focused on "eternal truths [that] are all spiritual things that are not seen with the eyes of the body, but with the eyes of the mind; that is, by reflection and consideration."[40] Just as the eyes look upon material things and can decipher their shape, color, and size, so must we pray and look at God's "eternal truths" to understand their meaning, significance, and impact upon our lives.

Meditation is a conversation in which our effort prevails—"a form of mental prayer in which the mind, in God's presence, thinks about God and divine things."[41] We seek to get to know God in

[40] Liguori, *Prayer*, 129.

[41] Fr. John Hardon, Modern Catholic Dictionary, s.v. "Meditation," Catholic Culture, https://www.catholicculture.org/culture/library/dictionary/index.cfm?id=34827.

Scripture and the lives of the saints; we ask relevant questions about God with our minds, and we actively pursue God with the faculty of our imagination. When considering the imagination, it's important to recognize that our meditation focuses on Jesus, who is the *image* of the Father and reveals the life of the Holy Trinity. In other words, Jesus *is* the *image* of our *image-ining*. Our meditation is not on arbitrary text but on the One the text describes and directs us to: Jesus Christ Himself.

Meditation is the "quest" and pursuit of God "to make our own in faith the subject considered, by confronting it with the reality of our own life" (CCC 2723). St. Alphonsus Liguori encourages us to use the eyes of our mind "to reflect and consider" the central place of the eternal truths in our lives, with its foundation as the Person of Jesus Christ.

Contemplation is a conversation that God initiates. The word *contemplation* is derived from the Latin *contemplatio*, or "the act of looking at." Interestingly, the Latin root of *contemplation* is *templum* (sacred). Accordingly, we could say that contemplation is simply looking at what is most sacred.

In contemplating the mysteries of God with the eyes of the heart the "looking at" moves to more of a "looking into"—the subtle movement of God that allows us to see Earth in light of Heaven; vocation in light of destiny; and otherwise ordinary moments in light of truth. "Looking into" Mary's Seven Sorrows can reveal divine truths in our lives.

Incidentally, the most sacred "looking into" is adoration of the Blessed Sacrament[42]—a contemplation in which intimacy is

[42] The word *adoration* comes from the Latin *adoratio*, derived from *ad ora* (to the mouth). Adoration is to be "mouth to mouth" with God, breathing in His life and love. In a sense, we could say that

shared between two friends. In the words of a peasant of Ars to St. John Vianney, explaining how he spent his time in front of the Blessed Sacrament: "I look at him and he looks at me" (see CCC 2715). Perhaps sometimes we find ourselves just looking at our spouses. As the years pass, and we get to know our spouses more, we discover looking at our spouses to be more potent than when we first met them; this is also true in our relationship and contemplation of Jesus and the inner life of the Trinity. Just as our hearts become absorbed by the presence of our spouses, so too our hearts become absorbed by the loving presence of the triune God. The more we get to know God, the more powerful our contemplation of God will be!

What is the distinction between contemplation and meditation? In meditation, while God is always present, we initiate our pursuit of God in the study of Scripture, doctrine, and so on. In contemplation, God is the primary mover; we do less as God steps in and does the work of quieting our soul—filling us with His consolation, light, and truth. Our pursuit of God in meditation ought to lead to our deeper contemplation of God—that more still, quiet gaze. What is found in meditation is tasted in contemplation—the goodness of God! The quest leads to enjoyment.

Does this enjoyment happen all the time? No. St. Alphonsus reminds us not to seek spiritual consolation as the sole fruit of our meditation. While it is true that God will bestow comfort to His beloved souls during meditation "to give them a foretaste of

---

the more we breathe in God, the better will we see into the ways God moves in our lives. In this sense, even a single look in adoration can be a powerful communication of love. In the words of St. Thérèse, "For me, prayer is a surge of the heart; it is a simple look turned toward heaven, it is a cry of recognition and of love, embracing both trial and joy" (CCC 2558).

the delights ... in Heaven,"[43] the reality is that many pious souls "experience dryness of spirit in meditation";[44] this dryness is a sharing in Christ's experience in the desert as a necessary means to their salvation. The period of dryness can yield the greatest rewards. When we seem to lack fervor, desire, and the ability to perform good deeds, we should embrace humility and acceptance. This state of meditation may prove to be more productive than others.[45] If our meditation leads to the absence of "feeling"—let our resolve be found in the deepest canyons of our hearts.

The Heart

"The paradise of God, so to say, is the heart of man," says St. Alphonsus.[46] Matters of the heart are often the very things that bring us the heartache, pain, and gut-wrenching experiences that keep us up late at night. While Liguori's words might not match our experience, we ought to listen when a Doctor speaks on matters of the heart.

The heart of every Christian is a heart of flesh but one that the Holy Spirit has penetrated. God tells the prophet Jeremiah that He will make a new covenant with His people: "I will put my law within them, and I will write it upon their hearts" (Jer. 31:33). We have not only God's law written in our hearts; we also have His Holy Spirit dwelling in our hearts. Every Christian heart is the dwelling place of the Holy Spirit, the dwelling place of God. Indeed, "the dwelling of God is with men" (Rev. 21:3).

43 Liguori, *Prayer*, 144.

44 Liguori, *Prayer*, 144.

45 See Liguori, *Prayer*, 144–145.

46 "The Paradise of God Is the Heart of Man," from the *Ascetical Works of St. Alphonsus Liguori*, Vatican website, https://www.vatican.va/spirit/documents/spirit_20010717_alfonso-liguori_en.html.

How do we keep paradise in our hearts? St. Alphonsus would have us consider the priority of the heart in our relationship with God. After all, is not the heart always preoccupied with relationships? Certainly, God is preoccupied with the heart: the heart is mentioned more than a thousand times in Sacred Scripture. Why? Because "it is the heart that prays.... It is the place of encounter" in our relationship with God (CCC 2562–2563). The heart is the seat of desire, and God's strongest desire is that we desire Him as much as He desires us. He anticipates your desire, waiting for you to speak, "to show you that He is near and is ready to listen to you and to console you."[47] When your heart speaks, it prays, entering deeper into God. This going deeper can take place only if the heart also listens. "God is not accustomed to speak to the soul that does not speak to Him."[48] Being unused to dealing with Him, such a soul will not understand His voice well when He speaks. Samuel did not say, "Lord, listen! Your servant is speaking" but, rather, "Speak, for thy servant is listening" (see 1 Sam. 3:10). Being in relationship with God is becoming "accustomed to talking to [God] face to face, familiarly, with confidence and love, as to a friend, the dearest friend you have, who loves you so much."[49] For this reason, prayer is never to be a static courtship with God but a love affair that sees every moment charged with eternal significance (see 1 Thess. 5:17).

For St. Alphonsus, the prayer of the heart speaks directly to God about our day-to-day affairs, "our business, our plans, our sorrows, our fears, and of all that concerns us."[50] And yes, that includes the pain and heartache mentioned above. God is concerned with

[47] "The Paradise of God."

[48] "The Paradise of God."

[49] "The Paradise of God."

[50] See "The Paradise of God."

every detail of our day. If we speak to God and listen to Him, we will grow familiar with His voice. The more fervently we pray, the more our hearts will pulse with the rhythm of God, moving to the pace of prayer.

The prayerful heart receives guidance from God. Have you ever experienced a tug on your heart that quietly advises you to go in an unexpected direction? Have you ever sensed the need to speak up when you wanted to stay quiet, or stay quiet when you wanted to speak up? These feelings can be promptings from the Holy Spirit, who desires to guide us in the right direction. Good promptings are often inspirations of the One who abides in the paradise that is your heart. The inspiration to pick up this book and pray the Chaplet of the Seven Sorrows of Mary is probably a prompting of the Holy Spirit.[51]

The heart is well-served when it conforms to the habit of prayer. This brings us to our next section on the importance of getting into the rhythm of structured daily prayer.

Meditation: A Habit in Time and Place

We hear the phrase "trust the process" in business and sports. While it sounds very cliche, in the context of faith and prayer it is another

[51] While this brief section focused on the heart's prayer, it is not to undermine the heart as the moral decision center. As Liguori examines in *Uniformity to God's Will*, our hearts must submit to a mature thinking process and a properly formed conscience based on Scripture and Church teaching. Otherwise, disordered feelings of selfishness, envy, anger, and so on can turn the paradise of our hearts into a living hell. We may face difficulties, even opposition, when we follow God's guidance. Discerning well gives us the confidence to hold fast to the direction we have received, knowing that we are following God's guidance in each situation. If we seek God, He will use everything, even our mistakes, to lead and guide us.

way of saying, "Let go and let God work." It is easier said than done when our progress is too small to be noticed. We tend to get frustrated with ourselves and God when we don't see God moving in the things we ask for, but as we have established, we are to understand that prayer is less about *asking for things* and more about *being in the presence of Someone and talking with that Someone, who is God.* If you are faithful in practicing the art of prayer, God will increase His blessing upon you by continually directing your heart to Him and protecting you from evil (see 2 Thess. 3:1–5). So "let not your heart be troubled" (see John 14:27) if you feel defeated in your practice of prayer. Begin again by taking the first step to reclaim your relationship with God—the step of making prayer a habit.

The habit of daily prayer is the first habit of being a Christian. Habits are notoriously hard to form and even harder to change once set. Making prayer a regular part of our day might be difficult to establish, especially if it means changing other habits. For example, we might be in the habit of waking up to our phones and scrolling through our social media threads before we thank God for the air we breathe. Or we might turn to the evening news instead of evening prayer. These habits might seem trivial, but if they are undoing the practice of prayer, they are dangerous to the soul.

We should regularly pause to take stock of our prayer lives, to see what might be replacing God. Far too often, we are left trying to *squeeze prayer into our busy schedules*, and often the result is that the busyness of our day *squeezes out prayer.* Do you have the best intentions to pray in the morning but sometimes forget? Do you intend to pray at bedtime and fall asleep as you start to pray? For prayer to be effective in our lives, it must be regular and habitual. It should be fully ingrained into the fabric of our lives, and when it is, it is free from monotony and boredom. "Conversation with God is not painful or tedious to those who truly love Him. His conversation has no bitterness, His company produces not tediousness, but joy and gladness."[52]

The first step in making mental prayer a habit involves setting aside specific times each day and ensuring that those times are filled with intentional prayer. In the words of St. Alphonsus, there are two aspects of time to consider: "the time of the day most suitable for mental prayer and the time spent in making it."[53] Just as married couples set aside time to go out on dates and fill that time with fellowship and joy, the person of prayer needs to set aside specific time with God and enter into the mystery of the eternal joy of the fellowship of the Trinity.

When should we pray? Echoing the Church Fathers, St. Alphonsus recommends setting aside blocks of time in the morning and in the evening. Why the morning? "When prayer precedes business, sin will not find entrance into the soul."[54] Like the body that grows weary without food in the morning, so does the soul grow weary without food. Let your soul gravitate to morning prayer as your body gravitates to breakfast (and coffee).

What is most important in the morning is that we begin our day by praising God and offering Him our day, including our works, joys, and sufferings. Morning Prayer is a great way to sanctify all the activities and works of our day.

We should also turn our hearts to God in the evening, for the body should not rest before being refreshed in mental prayer.[55] Fixed evening prayer puts us in the right frame of mind for the evening and nighttime hours. Satan abides in the dark, and we

[52] Liguori, *Prayer*, 152.
[53] Liguori, *Prayer*, 151.
[54] Liguori, *Prayer*, 151.
[55] Liguori, *Prayer*, 151.

must be vigilant in bringing light into those hours of darkness. Finishing our day with prayer is also a powerful way to let go of anxiety and find peace before falling asleep. What is more, praying in the evening is an opportunity to thank the Lord for the blessings and protection He has given us.

However we do it, the most important thing is that we do establish a habit of prayer—formal times to meditate upon our Beloved and how we might glorify Him in what we say and do. Again, the formal will bring all the informal moments into conversation with God. As St. Alphonsus states, through mental prayer the heart can pray "at all times and in all places."[56] In this sense, we can appreciate that prayer can happen "in every place, at home or elsewhere, even in walking and in working. How many are there who ... raise their hearts to God and apply their minds to mental prayer without leaving their purpose in occupation or work." In this, "the essential condition to converse with God is the solitude of the heart."[57]

Solitude is not mere isolation; it is intentional communion. As Jesus withdrew to the mountains to pray, we must withdraw to the solitude of our hearts to create space for God. Let us embrace that solitude, for within the heart's quiet chambers, we find the sacred meeting ground with the Almighty—where words are whispered, burdens are lifted, and souls are transformed. The solitude of the heart allows us to hear God even in the most unsuspecting places; "even in the public streets, in places of resort, and public assemblies can [we] possess a solitude of heart and continue united with God."[58] In the quiet of our hearts, we begin to see that the concreteness of our everyday life is charged with divine appointments.

[56] Liguori, *Prayer*, 151.
[57] Liguori, *Prayer*, 149.
[58] Liguori, *Prayer*, 149.

St. Alphonsus reminds us, however, that, as we are able, "we should retire to a solitary place to make our meditation,"[59] preferably before the Blessed Sacrament in adoration. "Jesus Christ especially delights in meditation that is made before the Blessed Sacrament."[60] We touched upon this above, but it stands repeating: this is the place of extraordinary intimacy with God—where lovers share their deepest affection for one another. There, Jesus "gives audience to all, hears all, and comforts all."[61]

We ought to see our homes as domestic outposts of our local parishes and should set up sacred spaces in our rooms. Jesus says, "When you pray, go into your room" (see Matt. 6:6), and so we do. We can set up in our bedrooms a table with a crucifix as our focal point. On that table we can place statues and prayer cards of the saints as reminders that we belong to a God who desires to meet us where we sleep and dress. We might also place on the table a candle that we can light when we pray, as a reminder that God's light belongs in all places. In this prayer area, we can invoke the presence of the Holy Spirit and begin to meditate.[62]

Three Steps to Better Meditation: Preparation, Meditation, and Conclusion

St. Alphonsus goes to great lengths to ensure that we understand that mental prayer should follow a rubric. If we are going to "enter into" the heart of Jesus in mental prayer, our hearts ought to be appropriately disposed. Liguori remarks that without the proper disposition, it will be impossible to hear the Lord speak to us.[63] For

[59] Liguori, *Prayer*, 150. Also, see Matthew 6:6.

[60] Liguori, *Prayer*, 150.

[61] Liguori, *Prayer*, 150.

[62] See Hollcraft, *Unleashing the Power of Intercessory Prayer*, 84–85.

[63] Liguori, *Prayer*, 153.

this reason, we should follow three steps for good mental prayer: the preparation, the meditation, and the conclusion.

Preparation

Preparation begins with sound recollection. As we enter our place of prayer, we should leave at the door all the noise and extraneous thoughts that have populated our minds.[64] In mental prayer, we first gather our hearts and "recollect our whole being under the prompting of the Holy Spirit" (CCC 2711). This recollection situates us "in the dwelling place of the Lord which we are and awakens our faith to enter into the presence of him who awaits us" (CCC 2711). Our recollected soul can then behold the One we know loves us, engaging in the intense "*gaze* of faith, fixed on Jesus" (CCC 2715).

Preparation includes the posture of the body. "The most suitable posture of the body is kneeling."[65] To pray is to beg, and to beg properly is to kneel. This is because the physical posture of kneeling is intended to express a spiritual attitude of adoration before the triune God; it is an act of humility, recognizing our littleness before God the Father. Kneeling prepares our hearts to receive God within our souls, striking down our pride with a physical reminder of what our souls should be like spiritually. For this reason, the Hebrews saw the knees as a symbol of strength; to bend the knee was to acknowledge strength—recognizing that all we are we owe to God.[66] Pope Benedict recounts a tale from the Desert Fathers, where the devil was compelled by God to reveal

[64] Liguori, *Prayer*, 153.

[65] Liguori, *Prayer*, 155.

[66] See Joseph Cardinal Ratzinger, *The Spirit of the Liturgy* (San Francisco: Ignatius Press, 2001), 191.

himself to a certain Abba Apollo. He appeared black and hideous, with odd-looking thin limbs, and most notably, he had no knees. Benedict points out that "the inability to kneel is considered the essence of the diabolical."[67]

Of course, kneeling is not always possible for every person or in every place, and in the end, any posture we can adopt that reflects authentic prayer of the heart is certainly acceptable to the Lord.

Once we have appropriately inclined our hearts and minds to God, we should make three acts that St. Alphonsus recommends to prepare our hearts and mind for meditation.[68]

Act of faith in the presence of God

My God, I believe that Thou art here present, and I adore Thee with my whole soul.

This prayer ought to be preceded by the prayer of the father whose son was possessed: "I believe; help my unbelief" (Mark 9:24). The conviction of lively faith arises from what has been received by our Father in Heaven and, in turn, given back to the Father in an act of trust; receiving the gift and acting in trust lead to more fervent prayer.

Incidentally, although this prayer was written in the mid-eighteenth century, one hundred years before the private revelations at Fátima, it points to the prayers that the angel taught the children at Fátima:

Most Holy Trinity—Father, Son and Holy Spirit—I adore Thee profoundly.

[67] See Ratzinger, *The Spirit of the Liturgy*, 193.

[68] These three prayers are taken from Liguori, *Prayer*, 156.

My God, I believe, I adore, I hope, and I love Thee.

I adore Thee! My God, my God, I love Thee in the Most Blessed Sacrament.

In other words, this act of faith in the presence of God is deeply Marian and unites our hearts with Our Lady of Sorrows. In fact, as we will see, each act of prayer, as laid out by Liguori, seem to anticipate Fátima.

Act of Humility and of Contrition

Lord, I should now be in Hell in punishment of the offenses I have given Thee. I am sorry for my sins from the bottom of my heart. I am firmly resolved with the help of your grace to sin no more and to avoid the near occasion of sin. Have mercy on me. Amen.

This prayer should remind us of our most recent confession and be a gauge for when we need to return to the sacrament. If we do not abide in the grace of the sacrament, we will lack genuine sorrow for our sins when we pray this prayer. It is the repentant heart that receives God's mercy.

This second prayer continues to unite us with the prayers that the angel taught the children at Fátima. There, the Blessed Mother stressed the importance of praying the Rosary daily for the conversion of sinners. She asked that the following prayer be recited at the end of each decade:

O my Jesus, forgive us our sins; save us from the fires of Hell; lead all souls to Heaven, especially those in most need of Thy mercy.

Just as we pray for a deeper sense of our sin and call out to God for His mercy upon us, so do we pray for all sinners and pray that God's mercy will flood each soul with grace.

Act of petition for light

Eternal Father, for the sake of Jesus and Mary, give me light in this meditation, that I may draw fruit from it. Amen.

This prayer has merit for us in praying with Our Lady of Sorrows because it invokes Mary's intercession. The phrase "*for the sake* of Jesus and Mary" is evocative of the Chaplet of Divine Mercy, in which we pray "*for the sake* of His sorrowful Passion." Mary is intimately united with her Son, and so we pray, "for the sake of her sorrowful passion." Every mother suffers when her child suffers. All the more did Mary suffer during her Son's Passion. Offering this act of prayer is another essential step in drawing light from Mary's Seven Sorrows.

Once again, the language of this prayer reflects the prayers at Fátima. On one occasion, the three children saw the angel prostrate himself before a host and chalice that hung in the air. Worshipping the Eucharist, the angel prayed:

Most Holy Trinity—Father, Son, and Holy Spirit—I adore Thee profoundly. I offer Thee the most precious Body, Blood, Soul, and Divinity of Jesus Christ, present in all the tabernacles of the world, in reparation for the outrages, sacrileges, and indifferences whereby He is offended. And through the infinite merits of His Most Sacred Heart and the Immaculate Heart of Mary, I beg of Thee the conversion of poor sinners.

Liguori's phrase "for the sake of" points to the fact that our meditation brings glory to the hearts of Jesus and Mary. The angel's prayer for "the conversion of poor sinners" is for the sake of God's glory: even the sin of man can be turned upside down and can lead to grace through redemptive suffering (see Rom. 5:20).

Meditation

As we move from preparation to meditation, let us not lose sight of what lies at the heart of our mental prayer: heart-to-heart contact with God. When we meditate upon the things of God, there will be moments, as in any courtship, when God, as our Beloved, will capture our hearts deeply. When He does, we need to stay there. Like the bee that draws nourishment from the flower until it has exhausted its offering, we should stay in that moment until God has finished feeding us.[69] Mental prayer is spiritual food; we should feast when the Holy Spirit desires to indulge us.

What do we meditate upon? We can find nourishment when reading a good spiritual book, sometimes pondering its content for a long time. Many of us have experienced reading a sentence, a paragraph, or a chapter of a book and finding ourselves mesmerized by how it spoke directly to our situation. Maybe we've even asked ourselves, "Did God just take what I'm reading and talk directly to me?" Typically, that happens when we invite the Holy Spirit into our mental prayer.

Books about Jesus and Mary can have an impact on us, but only one book has the actual words of Jesus and Mary: the Bible. Meditating upon verses in the Bible is the sweetest nectar the soul can find. For this reason, whatever book we read should always lead us to the Word of God. In it, we discover the most extraordinary sustenance. In this book, we will draw nourishment from the biblical passages tied to Mary's Seven Sorrows.

St. Alphonsus Liguori echoes the spiritual masters when he reminds us that "the advantage of mental prayer consists not so much in meditating as in making affections, petitions, and resolutions;

[69] Liguori, *Prayer*, 156.

these are the three principal fruits of meditation."[70] Let us look at each of these fruits in order that our meditations may nourish us and others.

Affections

In a world that is caught up with "love languages," when we hear the word *affection*, we often define it as a fondness or liking for someone and think of how we show our loved ones that we care for them. We put affection in the categories of spending money on our loved ones, giving hugs, saying nice things to one another, writing sweet notes, or, more generally, spending quality time with the objects of our affection. These are not all untrue with God, but what lies at the heart of the affections that arise from our mental prayer is the business of deep pious sentiments. These consist of "[raising] your heart to God and offering Him acts of humility, of confidence, or of thanksgiving; but, above all, [repeating] in mental prayer acts of contrition and of love."[71] "The act of love, as also the act of contrition … binds the soul to God."[72]

For Liguori, these acts of love, or offerings of the heart, are rooted in humility and find their growth in docility to the Holy Spirit, a disposition akin to humility. Here are some examples:[73]

My God, I desire You more than all things.

I love You with all my heart; I delight in Your joy.

I desire to see You loved above all else; my desire is Your desire.

[70] Liguori, *Prayer*, 157.

[71] Liguori, *Prayer*, 157.

[72] Liguori, *Prayer*, 158.

[73] These are paraphrases of Liguori's more classical Shakespearean way of speaking as seen on page 158 of his *Prayer*.

Make known what You desire from me, and I will do it.

Dispose of me as it pleases You and rid of me all earthly wants. Amen.

A particular grace is given to the soul in the last act of love, above, because such absolute surrender as "dispose of me as You wish" could conflict with how we think we should use our gifts and talents to serve the Church. Sometimes we are docile to the Spirit in discerning how to use our God-given gifts, but other times, where we think we are led is not where God is leading us. A young man or woman can get a postgraduate degree to assume a professorship but be surprised to find that God desires him or her to work in a place other than the classroom. Or the case might be altogether different; God might have led you to a particular place for an unforeseen reason—sometimes, the experiences along the way transform you and open unexpected doors. Other times, God might say, "Go there" when there is no rhyme or reason to do so. Jesus said to His apostles, "Go," and they went. Beyond Jesus' telling them to go, very little else made sense to them, but it didn't need to, and that's the genius of mental prayer! It is enough that the One we love said to us, "Go."

Now, if you should feel yourself "united with God by supernatural or infused recollection ... [you] should not then labor to perform any other acts than those to which [you feel yourself] sweetly drawn to God."[74] Here, Liguori wants us to be present to the spontaneity that abounds in any life-giving courtship. One of the wonders of courting another is the thrill of surprise. God loves to surprise us with His consolations. We should always leave room for that. We will fall more in love with Him if we do. But as this devotional is

[74] Liguori, *Prayer*, 159.

a structured way of praying with Mary's sorrows, we must always make room just to sit in God's presence when He says, "Be with me." Otherwise, we should follow the ordinary method of mental prayer, as prescribed by Liguori and the wisdom of the saints.[75]

Petitions

St. Alphonsus goes on to tell us that "all mental prayer should consist in acts and petitions," and that when presenting our other petitions to God we should ask "above all [for] the gift of His holy love."[76] Liguori stresses the importance of asking for God's holy love because to abide in His goodness is to abstain from anything that displeases Him. When we abide in Him, our petitions are more prompted and inspired by the grace of the Holy Spirit. Let this be our confidence; Jesus Himself told us, "Truly, truly, I say to you, if you ask anything of the Father, he will give it to you in my name" (John 16:23). "In my name" is another way of saying "abiding in my holy love." In His grace, His desire becomes our desire; our petitions are His inspirations.

The prayer of petition is more than just presenting requests; it's an active, personal dialogue with God, as Jesus encourages in Matthew 7:7 (ask, seek, knock). It involves our openness, vulnerability, and persistence. St. Alphonsus, referencing St. Gregory, says that God is "conquered by importunity" (zealous persistence), suggesting that our heartfelt prayers reach into the depths of God's heart.[77] Our perseverance not only brings us closer to God but also garners His response. The account of the Canaanite woman

[75] Liguori wants us to understand the importance of both the spontaneity and the structure.

[76] Liguori, *Prayer*, 160.

[77] Liguori, *Prayer*, 143.

in Matthew 15:21–28 exemplifies this. Jesus appears initially to dismiss her request, but her unwavering plea for her daughter's healing compels Jesus to act; He ultimately commends her faith and grants her request. This narrative serves as a poignant reminder that God values our steadfast trust and courage in approaching Him. Indeed, Jesus is "conquered by importunity."

Is there a "best time" to offer our petitions? Yes! In two of St. Paul's most famous exhortations to prayer, he tells us:

> First of all, then, I urge that supplications, prayers, intercessions, and thanksgivings be made for all men. (1 Tim. 2:1)

> Have no anxiety about anything, but in everything by prayer and supplication with thanksgiving let your requests be made known to God. (Phil. 4:6)

In these verses, the Greek term for "thanksgiving" is *eucharistia*, from which we get the word *eucharist*. The Eucharist is the place of union with God, and as Liguori reminds us, one of the beautiful fruits of our union with God ought to be the prayer of petition. In light of this, we should consider that praying the Chaplet of the Seven Sorrows before or after Mass might make it especially fruitful.

What's more, "intercession is a prayer of petition which leads us to pray as Jesus did" and share in His one mediation (see CCC 2634).

St. Paul writes to Timothy, "For there is one God, and there is one mediator between God and men, the man Christ Jesus" (1 Tim. 2:5). On the surface, this verse suggests that no one other than Christ is involved in mediation. What is a mediator? It is someone who resolves a conflict between parties. Theologically, a priest resolves a conflict between God and man (the conflict of sin). St. Paul refers to Christ as the "one mediator" because He, as the God-Man, perfectly resolved the conflict between God and man, once and for all; and He did so by sacrificing Himself on the Cross for the forgiveness of our sins. Therefore, Christ is the "one mediator," the one Priest, and the one sacrifice through which man's relationship with God is restored. And yet we are part of the Mystical Body of Christ. We are members of His Church, participating in this great work of redemption by virtue of our Baptism. By our prayers of intercession, we engage in this participation, in this work of redemption, with and through Christ. Only He is the perfect Mediator, but we are invited and called to share in this work (see 2 Pet. 1:4; Col. 1:24).

Furthermore, the quotation above from St. Paul can be better understood in its proper context. Just a few verses earlier, St. Paul urges prayers of intercession for the salvation of souls: "First of all, then, I urge that supplications, prayers, intercessions, and thanksgivings be made for all men.... This is good and it is acceptable in the sight of God our Savior, who desires all men to be saved and to come to the knowledge of the truth" (1 Tim. 2:1, 3–4). St. Paul writes "first" because the priority of the Church and the people of God is to pray. One mode of this prayer is to intercede with the help of the Holy Spirit. For St. Paul, it is clear that intercessory prayer through the one mediation of Jesus Christ is salvific, and it is something we are "urged" to carry out. Incidentally, the Greek word for "intercession" (1 Tim. 2:1) points to the intimate communion one shares with God, whereby the one praying enjoys favor with God to make a request. The Greek also connotes a drawing near to God *with an urgent need.* Indeed, this language of urgency ought to encourage us to pray the Chaplet of the Seven Sorrows of Mary daily and consistently.

God gives us the means to achieve His ends, and intercessory prayer is a means, or way, for us to share in His drawing all men to Himself. In the intercessory prayer that arises from deep union with God, we do not change God's mind, but we bring to fruition what is in God's mind. Our petitions order reality between us and God, and they accomplish something objective beyond ourselves. So, although it is true that the purpose of prayer is ultimately grounded in our relationship with God, through that prayer He also seeks to bring grace and healing to all His creation. This means that when we ask for something from a place of union with God, something is actually attained for our salvation and the salvation of the whole world. The Seven Sorrows Chaplet is a devotion that does bring about the healing of real wounds, wounds that are ugly and infected. Jesus desires to heal, to make all things new through our intercessory prayer. Our supplications and petitions unleash divine power that ought to renew hope—a hope that makes new the many parts of the Mystical Body of Christ!

Intercessory prayer allows us to imitate the men who carried their paralytic friend to Jesus for healing (see Mark 2:3–5). We are called to bring the needs of others before Jesus. Jesus said of a boy who needed healing, "Bring him to me" (Mark 9:19), and by praying the Chaplet of the Seven Sorrows with specific intentions, we answer Christ's call to bring to Him those who need His healing![78]

Resolutions

Meditation should always conclude with resolutions or a firm purpose of amendment—the determination to transform bad habits into good habits. *Resolution* is a word that resonates with many of us who live in North America, as we are accustomed to making New Year's resolutions.

The term *resolution* comes from the Latin *resolutio*, which means "to loosen" and speaks to a "process of reducing things into simpler

[78] For more on this topic of mediation and intercession, see Hollcraft, *Unleashing the Power of Intercessory Prayer*, 7–10.

forms." Our New Year's resolutions should take stock of that overarching proverb of *less* is *more*. We might make a resolution to lose weight because less physical weight may lead to more energy and an overall increase in self-esteem, but we are both body and soul. We could say the idea of "loosening" has as much to do with the need to root out some particular defect in our life as it does the "loosening" of our clothes as our waistlines grow thinner. We want less vice and more virtue. Whatever particular vice we struggle with, we should practice its counter-virtue. If we struggle with pride, we should practice humility; if we tend toward gossip, we should practice silence.

As we conclude our time in meditation, it is necessary to be sure we are making a firm purpose of amendment to identify our weaknesses and allow God's grace to transform those weaknesses into strengths. The more we receive God's grace in meditating upon Our Lord's and Our Lady's sorrows, the firmer our purpose will be to conform our lives to Christ.[79]

Conclusion

Finally, St. Alphonsus Liguori briefly touches upon the importance of concluding our meditation with three acts:

1. In thanking God for the lights received
2. In making a purpose to fulfill the resolutions made
3. In asking of the Eternal Father, for the sake of Jesus and Mary, grace to be faithful to them[80]

Alongside those acts, we should never omit from our prayers the souls in Purgatory and poor sinners.[81] We have been entrusted with

[79] Liguori, *Prayer*, 143.
[80] Liguori, *Prayer*, 143.
[81] Liguori, *Prayer*, 161.

helping those souls who have gone before us onward and upward into Heaven, especially those whom God has put into our paths in our lives. Being grateful for the lights God has granted us has a way of changing how we view the world and others. Even when things seem bleak, practicing gratitude helps us find the positive aspects of our circumstances. Gratitude turns what little we have into abundance. One of the sins against God is a lack of gratitude. Saying "thank you"—both sacramentally and in everyday life—helps build up our spiritual immune system against the viruses of Satan. Conversely, holding on to grudges weakens our spiritual immune system. Throughout our day, we should reflect on one or two things that God has done for us. This will deepen our love for our heavenly Father and perhaps provide points for future meditations.

Mental Prayer: Avoid Distractions

Often, the biggest stumbling block to our mental prayer is the distractions that easily pull our attention away from Jesus. St. Alphonsus encourages us not to be disturbed by distractions but to "remove [them] calmy and return to God."[82]

The *Catechism of the Catholic Church* reminds us that distractions reveal to us "what we are attached to" (2729). Something as simple as our daily to-do list can sometimes feel like a tsunami of stress and activity, but more often, as the *Catechism* states, our wandering minds tend to gravitate toward those things we are most attached to: the sports team we are rooting for, the song-and-dance competition we watched last night, or maybe something more serious, such as the seemingly broken relationship that feels unfixable. Whatever distracts us, the important thing is to remove it as a distraction in our meditation.

[82] Liguori, *Prayer*, 163.

And what is the means for doing this? It is Jesus. In our meditation, we have found it very beneficial to take the very thing that pulls us sideways in our prayer and entrust it to Jesus—this can be a powerful way of reorienting our meditation on Jesus. If our distraction is all the errands we have to do, place the essential errands before Jesus. If our distraction is an unhealthy attachment to a sports team or a television show, let Jesus squash that out. If our distraction is a friend who has betrayed us, entrust that situation to the Most Sacred Heart of Jesus for healing to take place. By giving our distractions, big or small, to Jesus, we simultaneously take them out of our hands.

However we may deal with our distractions, we must never give up on meditation, no matter how great our distractions may be.[83] Indeed, distractions are a ploy of the devil.

We saw earlier that the word *devil* comes from the Greek *diaballein*, which means "to throw across or to scatter." When we are distracted, our hearts are scattered. The "pure of heart … see God" (Matt. 5:8) because they are singularly focused on Jesus. Purity is derived from a Greek word that means "single-hearted" (more on this later). To pull our attention away from Jesus, the devil tries to preoccupy our minds with nonessential matters (such as the team we root for or the show we dwell on) or concerns we have that we cannot control (such as a friend's negative response to something we have said or done).

Indeed, the devil employs cunning strategies to lead us astray and divert our focus from God. One of his most successful tricks is to convince us that he does not exist. Another is to entice us to believe that we can solve life's problems independently, without God's intervention. The ancient temptation in the Garden of

[83] Liguori, *Prayer*, 163.

Eden echoes this truth. The serpent whispered to Eve, "You can be like God." This enticing lie distracts us from our dependence on God and fosters self-reliance, which distances us from God. And to distance us from God—away from light, into the abysmal darkness—is Satan's end game.

For this reason, let us heed St. Paul's recommendation to make our requests known to God so that His peace may pervade our souls and protect our minds and hearts in Christ Jesus (see Phil. 4:6–7). Offering intercessory prayer during our meditation can lead to a great triumph over the devil's attempts to divert our focus on Jesus.

What's more, we need Mary in this spiritual warfare with the devil!

Dear readers, "the devil labors hard to disturb us in the time of meditation, in order to make us abandon it,"[84] but we have been given a particular gift, which is Mary, who crushes the head of the serpent (see Gen. 3:15). Mary is our victory and remembering that truth will serve us well in our meditation. Mary lived the entirety of her life without ever pulling her eyes away from Jesus. She can help us to focus on Jesus in our meditation. Again, Mary's pondering (*symballein*) was one of intense focus and concentration, constantly "bringing together" or "making sense of" the life of Christ.

Contemplation: The Indispensable Beholding

In our reflection on mental prayer, we noted that contemplation is a gaze shared between two lovers—in which we continuously hold in view the one who has captured our hearts. We behold Jesus, and Jesus behold us. In this beholding, Jesus keeps, protects, and even saves us because only when we first contemplate Jesus *as He is* do we begin to work out our salvation "with fear and trembling"

[84] Liguori, *Prayer*, 163.

(Phil. 2:12). This is the importance of beholding Jesus; this is the importance of contemplation.

In light of this, it should be no surprise that the word *behold* can be found more than twelve hundred times in Sacred Scripture, where it is rich with meaning. In the Old Testament, the most common word for *behold* is *hinneh*, which is used as an introduction to something new and unexpected. In the New Testament, *behold* primarily comes from the Greek *idou*, which invites perception and a deeper consideration of what follows. At its center, the word *behold* in the Bible is an exclamation that draws attention to something important. It signals the reader to pause, take notice, and carefully consider what follows, often a stunning revelation. The word reflects a sense of wonder and awe at the works and words of God. To behold is first to see, then to search with excitement and intensity, and finally, to understand. In this, beholding is an invitation to worship, contemplate, and respond.

So we are called to behold Jesus, but is there something specific to Jesus we should focus on? And does this particularity have anything to do with Mary and her experience with sorrow? To both questions, we suggest, yes! Let's consider.

In the first use of the word *behold* in the Gospel of John, St. John the Baptist, upon seeing Jesus coming toward him, says: "Behold, the Lamb of God, who takes away the sins of the world!" (1:29). With this initial usage of *behold* by St. John the Baptist, we are encouraged to look upon Jesus with intensity, to search for meaning in His identity as the Lamb of God, and so to understand His mission to save us.

Incidentally, the title "Lamb of God" would have resonated powerfully with the first-century Jews. A reference to the Lamb of God would have also drawn their attention to the Temple. The Temple is where the Jews brought the lambs to be slain and sacrificed. Here, let us remember our initial breakdown of the word *contemplation* and that the word *templum* is its root. Let's probe further. The word *temple* has the root *tem*, "to cut," in reference to a place reserved or "cut out" for worship. What we understand as a "cutting out" or "stretching" in terms of a space cleared in front of an altar could also be a reflection of Jesus, who was "cut up" and "stretched" on the altar of the Cross—which makes possible the new space where we are called to offer our worship to God.

So what are we to behold? Christ crucified (see 1 Cor. 1:23; 2:2)! We follow the cue of Pontius Pilate, "Behold, the man" (*Ecce Homo*) (see John 19:5). In beholding Christ crucified, we "look into" His wounds of love and, in doing so, search for the great meaning of Christ's love and tireless mercy, which leave us stunned. If we want to contemplate the wounds of Jesus, we must also contemplate our wounds because they belong to Him. Of course, the wounds of Jesus are more and greater, but that is because His wounds must cover every wound in human history. Your wounds are His!

Some may hesitate, thinking, "I just don't know. I can't let Him into *that* space or *that* wound." We all have our sorrowful mysteries. There is no aspect of our life that God does not care about. He desires to fill your soul completely! Christianity is about liberation, not managing wounds. When God observes our wound, He sees pain. He grants us freedom from burdens we don't even realize we carry. God doesn't coerce us into conversion; He loves us into freedom, cherishing every part of us. As parents often say to their children, "I just love you to pieces!" Similarly, God adores every piece of us, loving us into being.

Healing is a continuous encounter with God, in which He, as the supreme storyteller, speaks into our story. God looks into our past and declares, "I have always been there; welcome me into that space you have neglected. You call it *history* because every *story* is

His–mine!" God looks into the present and declares, "Instead of merely living for the moment, exist within it, acknowledging its potential and obstacles. This moment is the time for prayer, a time of grace, where your distinct narrative will shine bright in my love!" God looks into our future and perceives the yet-to-be-written chapters of our stories, eager as the most enthralled reader for the unfolding events that are still to come. He beholds us, and so we behold Him.

As we behold Christ on the Cross, we are reminded of two beholdings: "When Jesus saw his mother, and the disciple whom he loved standing near, he said to his mother, 'Woman, behold, your son!' Then he said to the disciple, 'Behold, your mother!' And from that hour the disciple took her to his own home" (John 19:26–27). Jesus asks Mary to behold us, which in itself is an extraordinary thing—that Mary never takes her eyes off us. Mary's fixed and penetrating gaze upon us ought to be enough for us to desire to be with her, to want to accompany her in her spiritual crucifixion on Calvary. The indispensable beholding is of Christ crucified, and that leads to the mutual beholding between the sorrowful heart of Mary and her child.

Beholding Movements of the Heart

The genius of Our Lady in requesting that we pray the Seven Sorrows Chaplet is directly related to this beholding, as the loving gaze is like a portal into the mind and heart of Mary and what she experienced in the Seven Sorrows. To behold is to get into the secrets of Mary's Immaculate Heart and the mysteries that await us as she looks to minister to us in our needs. Why? Because the prayers of the righteous soul avail much (see James 5:16). The more we learn from her, the more we will be present to her in her sorrows.

We encourage you to consider seven possible movements of the heart that emerge from the biblical text for each of the seven sorrows. While we read these movements of the heart as fruits of our meditation, we recognize that the Lord might stir up other movements in our hearts. Our meditations are not the "summa" for your prayer but only a starting point. Be sure to follow the Spirit's lead in your prayer.

Below are some possible movements of the heart. As you read them, be attentive to how Mary might challenge you in your relationship with her Son.

First Sorrow—The Prophecy of Simeon: Surrender to God's providence, following Mary's example.

Second Sorrow—The Flight into Egypt: The Word of God is living and breathing. As you invite the Holy Spirit into your reading of the text, allow the power of God to transform your heart and to direct the significant and the seemingly insignificant decisions of your life.

Third Sorrow—The Loss of the Child Jesus in the Temple: Let your heart be continually repentant and never cease pursuing Christ.

Fourth Sorrow—The Meeting of Mary and Jesus on the Way to Calvary: Always be present to those in need and willing to meet them where they are in their walk with God, no matter the cost.

Fifth Sorrow—The Crucifixion: Pray for a strong, immovable faith in the healing and restoration you can receive only from Christ Our Lord.

Sixth Sorrow—Mary Receives the Body of Jesus in Her Arms: Be continually open to the divine indwelling, receiving what Christ desires to give you.

Seventh Sorrow–The Burial of Jesus: Be available to God and your neighbor by fulfilling your duties toward them.

Vocal Prayer

Vocal prayer is prayer in word, action, and bodily posture. Since we are composed of soul and body, we must use our minds, our bodies, and our senses to enter fully into the mystery of vocal prayer. "We must pray with our whole being to give all power possible to our supplication" (CCC 2702). In vocal prayer, we express our interior inspirations and reverence for God in articulated words and bodily posture—this is seen most profoundly in the Mass as we pray out loud while kneeling, standing, bowing, or gesturing with our hands.

In vocal prayer, it is common to pray in formal words, such as the Rosary, the Divine Office, or the Chaplet of the Seven Sorrows of Mary. It might be your experience to pray vocal prayers superficially, without concentrating on the words you say aloud. Here, we have found it helpful to begin all our prayers with an invocation to the Holy Spirit so that our audible words might be imbued and inspired with His love. As the Holy Spirit brings us into the presence of God, He assists us in our focus and concentration.

The Holy Spirit is also like a spiritual GPS, setting our vocal prayer along the path toward Heaven. And this GPS, fixing our prayer in a particular direction, is also an instrument to see the depths of the mysteries we pray. Understanding the mysteries is essential to staying on the path toward Heaven.

Vocal prayer also includes expressing ourselves audibly in those more spontaneous moments of life. Consider that Jesus "raised his voice to express his personal prayer, from exultant blessing of the Father to the agony of Gethsemani" (CCC 2701). In Gethsemani, Jesus teaches us that vocal prayer includes the heart's cries.

God always answers such vocal prayer because He always has the optimal good in mind as a response to our prayer. Whatever the circumstances, God is always in the business of strengthening His people. We can cry out to Him, knowing that He will hear us, answer our prayers, and send us the strength we need to endure. "Let us then with confidence draw near to the throne of grace, that we may receive mercy and find grace to help in time of need" (Heb. 4:16). Again, when we cry out to God, we are not calling out to a distant deity. We call upon the God who created us, designed us for relationship, and desires to hear and answer our prayers. Vocal prayer is a powerful means of setting in motion the power of God in our lives.

Now, a word about understanding the distinction between vocal prayer and mental prayer as it relates to the practice of the Seven Sorrows of Mary. The Chaplet of the Seven Sorrows is a vocal prayer that is a form of mental prayer, as it requires the engagement of both mind and heart to be effective. The devotion orients our minds and hearts on the prayers of the chaplet and on the sorrowful dimension of Mary's life; and it often enriches our other times of mental prayer.

We encourage you to spend additional time with God in deeper mental prayer: uniting heart and mind with God and getting to know Jesus in the Gospels. This deeper orientation is centered on the encounter with God, engaging in a personal dialogue with Him. It is through this lively conversation that we come to know and love Jesus. In practice, these are stirrings of the heart that emerge from silence and friendship with Him. Remember all that has been said about mental prayer; it cultivates a dedication to live as Jesus did. It is the pathway through which we aspire to sainthood. The end goal of mental prayer is that we would live and act according to our heart-to-heart encounters with Jesus.

4

PROMISES, PROMISES

What Is Behind a Promise from God?

In a vision to St. Bridget of Sweden, the Blessed Virgin Mary appeared with the holy prophet Simeon and an angel bearing a long sword red with blood. In that vision, Mary revealed that she would grant particular graces to those who honor her daily with seven Hail Marys while meditating upon her tears and sorrows:

1. I will grant peace to their families.
2. They will be enlightened about the divine mysteries.
3. I will console them in their pains, and I will accompany them in their work.
4. I will give them as much as they ask for, as long as it does not oppose the adorable will of my divine Son or the sanctification of their souls.
5. I will defend them in their spiritual battles with the infernal enemy, and I will protect them at every instant of their lives.
6. I will visibly help them at the moment of their death—they will see the face of their mother.
7. I have obtained this grace from my Son, that those who propagate this devotion to my tears and sorrows

> will be taken directly from this earthly life to eternal happiness, since all their sins will be forgiven and my Son will be their eternal consolation and joy.

Although man tends to be fickle in following through on promises, when God sends someone to earth and lays out a set of promises with specific guidelines, we can be assured He will keep His promise—if we follow those guidelines.

The promises of God are a central theme in Sacred Scripture. They serve as a source of hope, a foundation for faith, and a guide for our prayer lives. In the Bible, a promise reveals a truth that benefits us—what God will bless us with or remove from us.

God's promises come in various forms: conditional and unconditional. Conditional promises depend on our obedience or response, while unconditional promises are based solely on God's faithfulness. Examples of conditional promises include blessings for obedience (see Prov. 16:20; 28:14); unconditional promises include God's covenants with Noah (see Gen. 9:8–17), Abraham (see Gen. 12:1–3), and David (see 2 Sam. 7:10–17).

Incidentally, in Sacred Scripture, the number seven is tied to fulfilling God's promise and oaths, which is incumbent upon us to consider, given that we are praying with Mary's *Seven* Sorrows.

The number seven is significant in the Bible, appearing more than seven hundred times. Foundational to understanding why seven is so substantial can be found in Genesis 21:27–31 and the covenant between Abraham and Abimelech in Beersheba. *Beersheba* means "the well of seven" or "the well of the oath." The name is derived from the Hebrew words *be'er* (meaning "well") and *sheva* (meaning "seven" or "oath"). Abraham dug a well and named it Beersheba because he and Abimelech made an oath there. Seven ewe lambs were offered in sacrifice during this event, and that is why the name is associated with the number seven. The Hebrew root *shabha* means both "to swear" and "to come under the influence of seven." In the covenant made between Abimelech and Abraham, animals were exchanged for something: "this is yours, and this is mine." In the covenants made between God and man in salvation history (with Adam, Noah, Abraham, Moses, and David), the language was made personal: "I am yours, and you are mine." From Adam to David, the exchange of persons between God and man culminates in the fulfillment of God's promises in and through Christ. The number seven is seen so frequently in the bible because the Bible is a book about God's radical love for man. Whether it be Elisha instructing Naaman to wash seven times in the Jordan River for healing (see 2 Kings 5:10), God protecting Cain by declaring that anyone who harms him will suffer vengeance sevenfold (see Gen. 4:15), or Jesus using seven metaphors to describe Himself as the path to salvation, God is constant in His reminder of His desire to be in covenant relationship with man.

We can begin to appreciate why seven is so relevant in the life of the Church and her devotional practices.[85] Consider:

- Seven sacraments: The Latin word for *sacrament* is *sacramentum*, meaning "oath." Sacraments are outward signs

[85] The book of Leviticus defines the significance of 7 sets of 7. The Year of Jubilee was the sabbatical year after 7 cycles of 7 years, or 49 years. The 50th year was a time full of rejoicing and celebration for Israel because both the people and the land were given a rest period. A set of 7 is called a "septet." The Seven Sorrows Chaplet has 7 sets of septets, which is 49. The number 49 is significant because it represents the number of years between each jubilee year. The angel Gabriel, who heard Mary's yes, had not been seen for 490 years when he told the prophet Daniel that it would be 490 years until the coming of the Messiah (see Dan. 9:24–27).

that convey invisible spiritual realities. God imparts sanctifying grace to our souls through the sacraments, transforming and sanctifying us. In the sacraments, we are incorporated into the Mystical Body of Christ and sustained as sons and daughters of God in God's providential care. Our stories as baptized people are revelations of God's fulfillment of His promise.

- Seven gifts of the Holy Spirit: In the sacrament of Confirmation, we receive the seven gifts of the Holy Spirit: wisdom, understanding, counsel, fortitude, knowledge, piety, and fear of the Lord. These gifts empower us to live virtuously and draw closer to God—shaping and forming our stories as echoes of God's great promise.
- Seven last words of Jesus: During His Crucifixion, Jesus spoke seven last words from the Cross (Luke 23:34, 43; John 19:26–27; Matt. 27:46; John 19:28, 30; Luke 23:46). These words reveal His love, forgiveness, and sacrifice for humanity—sealing His promise that He would be with us always.
- Seven in the book of Revelation: The book of Revelation speaks of seven seals, seven trumpets, and seven bowls. These symbolize God's Final Judgment and the culmination of human history—pointing us to the one great promise of eternal communion with Him.

In summary, the number seven in Sacred Scripture and Catholicism represents divine perfection, healing, spiritual completeness, and God's continued presence in our lives—always pointing to a Father who keeps His promises. We must understand that God's promises are grounded in His unchanging love, faithfulness, and sovereignty. They are a sure foundation for our hope and the object of our faith.

Through Mary, God gave us seven promises, and we can be assured that God will hold up His end of the bargain, but what about us? What are the prerequisites for us? These promises are not a get-out-of-Hell-free card.

Our End of the Bargain

If the disposition of our hearts is not correct, the mere recitation of endless chaplets, Rosaries, or any other devotional practices will not help us. Jesus told us that if we love Him, we will keep His commandments. It stands to reason that if we say we love Mary, we will also do as she asked us. So we need to avoid the danger of practicing a devotion such as the Chaplet of the Seven Sorrows without first living what the devotion requires of us.

Fulfilling our end of the bargain starts with our pursuit of holiness and living a life of conversion.

Holiness involves walking humbly in the presence of God. Humility involves having a modest estimate of one's self-worth before God and others, for God's sake, and this is achievable only through God's grace. In other words, humility involves thinking less about ourselves rather than having a lesser opinion of ourselves. How do we cultivate humility? In prayer, Scripture study, frequent Confession and Mass, and serving others in the works of mercy—this is the genius of Catholicism!

Humility is the fountainhead of all good mental prayer. As discussed in the opening chapters, prayer is a sacred conversation with God that includes supplication, petition, adoration, gratitude, and guidance. As a child approaches his father, we approach God the Father. Prayer increases our trust in God's plan for us and prompts us to surrender to God. Trust is essential to a life of holiness. "Set your minds on things that are above, not on things that are on earth" (Col. 3:2). Our instincts may drive us to hold on to control, but letting go is what leads to personal growth, healing, and a deeper awareness of God's presence in our hearts. Often, the very aspect of our lives we are most reluctant to relinquish to God is precisely what He most desires from us. We might worry, "If I give up this, what will happen to me?" Yet, in this leap of faith, He is ready to catch us.

Mental prayer also includes reading Sacred Scripture and getting to know the One we are conversing with. The Bible is the story of God's love for man—the more we study Scripture, the more we fall in love with God. In that same vein, the more we meditate on Our Lady's sorrows, the more insight we receive into Our Lord's graces.

The sacraments are those essential, intimate encounters with God in which we receive His grace and are nourished in His love, His Holiness. In this holiness, we live in His outgoing mercy and love—in deed (corporal works of mercy) and word (spiritual works of mercy). Holiness is not about giving up what's "fun" in life but finding complete fulfillment in God by practicing the art of living in Him and existing for others.

Finally, holiness is about constant conversion. Conversion comes from the Latin word *conversio*, meaning "to turn around." In the New Testament, the Greek term *metanoia* signifies a change of heart, particularly toward repentance. Conversion encompasses turning from sin to repentance, shifting from laxity to fervor, and embracing moral virtue over vice. Identifying sinful areas in our lives is not a one-time event but a daily choice to turn toward God and continually deepen our faith. Through obedience to God in our daily living, we are more ready to hold up our end of the bargain.

Liguori's Promises

There are four additional promises that St. Alphonsus Liguori provides for us that echo the seven that Mary gave to St. Bridget of Sweden:

1. That those, who before death, invoke the Divine Mother, in the name of her sorrows, should obtain true repentance for all their sins.
2. That [Jesus] would protect all who have this devotion in their tribulations, and that He would protect them especially at the hour of death.
3. That He would impress upon their minds the remembrance of His Passion, that they should have their reward for it in Heaven.
4. That He would commit such devout clients to the hands of Mary, with the power to dispose of them in whatever manner she might please, and to obtain for them all the graces she might desire.[86]

A Closing Word

St. Simeon received the promise that he would not die until he had seen the Messiah of the Lord. But this grace was obtained only through Mary, for he was handed the Savior from her arms. Hence, he who desires to find Jesus will not find Him other than through Mary. Let us then do as our Mother asks of us. She has sacrificed everything for us. And she wishes to give us what is promised to us. If we provide it with a heart full of love and genuine devotion, we will find that Jesus and Mary are ours forever!

Our Lady has repeatedly asked us to have compassion on her by remembering and accompanying her in the Chaplet of the Seven Sorrows. The Seven Sorrows Chaplet places us into the moment of each of Mary's seven major sorrows, walking with her through each event as her close friend, as the "other Marys" did at Calvary. Are we praying with her? Consoling her? If we do not,

[86] Liguori, *The Glories of Mary*, 588.

who will? Compassion without action is just an observation. Our Lady promises to soften your heart, inclining the ear of your heart with hers, transforming your heart into a heart that belongs to her. Through this devotion, your heart will know her grief intimately and the deep sorrow of her Son. Will you spend a little time with her? Let this be your promise to her!

In venerating Our Lady of Sorrows, in comforting and consoling her in her sufferings, past and present, we are also extending God's glory and love to all people. Through our cooperation with our Lady's mission and mandate, we are thereby extending her mantle of protection upon those whom we pray for.

5

HOW TO PRAY THE CHAPLET

HOW TO PRAY

THE CHAPLET OF THE SEVEN SORROWS OF MARY

The diagram to the right shows the numbers that correspond to each prayer or set of prayers. Each set of seven beads, which begins with a separate bead, is called a "septet."

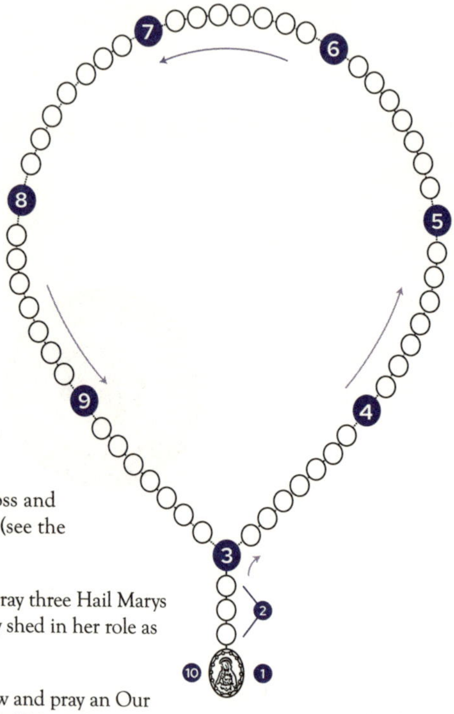

1. Make the Sign of the Cross and pray the opening prayers (see the following page).

2. On the first three beads: pray three Hail Marys in honor of the tears Mary shed in her role as Christ's Mother and ours.

3. Announce the First Sorrow and pray an Our Father. Then pray seven Hail Marys (one for each bead), adding the specified petition for that sorrow (see the following pages). Each added petition begins with "obtain for me the grace of," a favorite phrase of St. Alphonsus Liguori when praying to Mary. After each septet of Hail Marys, pray the closing prayer for that septet.

4-9 Repeat the same sequence for the Second through Seventh Sorrows.

10 Pray the concluding prayers and make the Sign of the Cross.

PRAYERS OF THE CHAPLET

Sign of the Cross

Opening Prayers

O my Jesus, I am sorry for my sins from the bottom of my heart. I am firmly resolved with the help of Your grace to sin no more and to avoid the near occasion of sin. Have mercy on me. Amen.

Eternal Father, I own and accept all my sufferings, sorrows, and trials, uniting them with merits of Christ's Passion and Death, along with the sufferings of Our Lady of Sorrows, offering them to You, that they may accomplish their purpose for Your glory. I offer them in consolation and reparation for sin, and the rejection and offenses committed against the Sacred Heart of Jesus and the Sorrowful and Immaculate Heart of Mary. Grant that I might worthily praise Our Lord Jesus in and through Your most Holy Mother by these prayers.

Eternal Father, for the sake of Jesus and Mary, give me light in this meditation, that I may draw fruit from it. Amen.

My special intention for this chaplet is: ________.

FIRST SORROW: THE PROPHECY OF SIMEON

Key patron: St. Dymphna and the sorrow of increasing mental illness

Our Father, who art in Heaven, hallowed be Thy name. Thy kingdom come; Thy will be done on earth as it is in Heaven. Give us this day our daily bread, and forgive us our trespasses as we forgive those who trespass against us. And lead us not into temptation, but deliver us from evil. Amen.

Hail Mary, full of grace, the Lord is with thee. Blessed art thou among women, and blessed is the fruit of thy womb, Jesus. Holy Mary, Mother of God, pray for us sinners, **obtain for me the grace of a heart united with thee in thy sorrows**, now and at the hour of our death. Amen. (*seven times*)

Closing Prayer

Blessed Mother, it is not with one sword only that I have pierced your heart, but I have done so with as many as are the sins which I have committed. Since you have been pleased to suffer so much for me, by your merits, obtain for me great sorrow for my sins and patience under the trials of this life, which will always be light in comparison to my sins. Amen.[87]

[87] Liguori, *The Glories of Mary*, 415.

SECOND SORROW: THE FLIGHT INTO EGYPT

Key patron: St. Joseph and the sorrow of the broken family

Our Father …

Hail Mary, full of grace, the Lord is with thee. Blessed art thou among women, and blessed is the fruit of thy womb, Jesus. Holy Mary, Mother of God, pray for us sinners, **obtain for me the grace of a heart for obedience in all things**, now and at the hour of our death. Amen. (*seven times*)

Closing Prayer

O Mary, even after your Son died by the hands of men who persecuted Him unto death, these ungrateful men have not yet ceased to persecute Him by their sins and continue to afflict you, O Sorrowful Mother! My most sweet Mother, obtain for me the tears to weep over such ingratitude. By the sufferings you endured in your journey to Egypt, assist me in the journey to which I am now engaged towards eternity; that I may one day be united with you in loving my persecuted Savior in the kingdom of the blessed. Amen.[88]

[88] Liguori, *The Glories of Mary*, 421.

THIRD SORROW: THE LOSS OF THE CHILD JESUS IN THE TEMPLE

Key patron: St. Josephine Bakhita and the sorrow of human trafficking

Our Father . . .

Hail Mary, full of grace, the Lord is with thee. Blessed art thou among women, and blessed is the fruit of thy womb, Jesus. Holy Mary, Mother of God, pray for us sinners, **obtain for me the grace of a heart that steadfastly searches and calls for Christ**, now and at the hour of our death. Amen. (*seven times*)

Closing Prayer

Most amiable Mother, leave sighs and groanings to me, and to so many sinners who love Him not, and who have lost Him by offending Him. I know only too well that He is found by those who seek Him. Dearest Mother, make me seek Him as I ought, for you are the gate through which all find Jesus; through you I also hope to find Him. Amen.[89]

[89] Liguori, *The Glories of Mary*, 426.

FOURTH SORROW: THE MEETING OF JESUS AND MARY ON THE WAY TO CALVARY

Key patron: Bl. Pier Giorgio Frassati and the sorrow of youth losing their identity

Our Father . . .

Hail Mary, full of grace, the Lord is with thee. Blessed art thou among women, and blessed is the fruit of thy womb, Jesus. Holy Mary, Mother of God, pray for us sinners, **obtain for me the grace to unselfishly meet the needs of others**, now and at the hour of our death. Amen. (*seven times*)

Closing Prayer

My sorrowful Mother, by the merits of that grief which you felt at seeing your beloved Jesus led to death, obtain for me the grace that I may also bear with patience the crosses that God sends me. Happy, indeed, will I be if I only know how to accompany you with my cross until death. Amen.[90]

[90] Liguori, *The Glories of Mary*, 432.

FIFTH SORROW: THE CRUCIFIXION

Key patron: Bl. Bartolo Longo and the sorrow of the rise of the occult

Our Father . . .

Hail Mary, full of grace, the Lord is with thee. Blessed art thou among women, and blessed is the fruit of thy womb, Jesus. Holy Mary, Mother of God, pray for us sinners, **obtain for me the grace of a strong faith that stands unmoved, in suffering and loss**, now and at the hour of our death. Amen. (*seven times*)

Closing Prayer

Dearest Mother, most sorrowful of all mothers, who can ever console you? The thought of what your Son Jesus has gained in conquering Hell, opening Heaven, and gaining so many souls in whose heart He reigns . . . this alone can console you. Be pleased to keep me near to you, to weep with you, since I have so much reason to weep for the crimes by which I have offended Him. Mother of Mercy, I hope through the death of my Redeemer, and through your bitter sorrows, to obtain pardon and eternal salvation. Amen.[91]

[91] Liguori, *The Glories of Mary*, 439.

SIXTH SORROW: MARY RECEIVES THE BODY OF JESUS IN HER ARMS

Key patron: St. Maria Goretti and the sorrow of our hypersexualized culture

Our Father ...

Hail Mary, full of grace, the Lord is with thee. Blessed art thou among women, and blessed is the fruit of thy womb, Jesus. Holy Mary, Mother of God, pray for us sinners, **obtain for me the grace of a pure and receptive heart**, now and at the hour of our death. Amen. (*seven times*)

Closing Prayer

O afflicted Virgin, my Mother, pity me, for instead of loving God, I have greatly offended Him. Your sorrows encourage me to hope for pardon. But this is not enough; I wish to love my Lord; and who can better obtain for me this love than you, who are the Mother of fair love? Mary, you comfort everyone; console me also. Amen.[92]

[92] Liguori, *The Glories of Mary*, 445.

SEVENTH SORROW: THE BURIAL OF JESUS

Key patron: St. Hildegard of Bingen and the sorrow of Christ, the Good Shepherd

Our Father …

Hail Mary, full of grace, the Lord is with thee. Blessed art thou among women, and blessed is the fruit of thy womb, Jesus. Holy Mary, Mother of God, pray for us sinners, **obtain for me the grace of a heart that ponders Christ's Passion and thine**, now and at the hour of our death. Amen. (*seven times*)

Closing Prayer

My afflicted Mother, I will not leave you alone to weep; no, I will accompany you with my tears. This grace I now ask of you; that I may always bear in mind and have a tender devotion toward the Passion of Jesus, and your sorrows, that all my life I will weep over your sufferings and those of my Redeemer. Obtain for me pardon, perseverance, and Heaven, where I hope to rejoice with you and sing the infinite mercies of my God for all eternity. This I do hope, this may it be. Amen.[93]

[93] Liguori, *The Glories of Mary*, 450.

Concluding Prayers

Mary, Queen of Martyrs, your heart suffers so much. I beg you by the merits of the tears you shed in these terrible and sorrowful times, to obtain for me the grace of complete sincerity and repentance. Amen.

Mary, who was conceived without sin, and who suffered for us, pray for us. (*three times*)

Sign of the Cross

6

MEDITATIONS ON THE CHAPLET OF THE SEVEN SORROWS

First Sorrow

THE PROPHECY OF SIMEON

Luke 2:22–38

And when the time came for their purification according to the law of Moses, they brought him up to Jerusalem to present him to the Lord (as it is written in the law of the Lord, "Every male that opens the womb shall be called holy to the Lord") and to offer a sacrifice according to what is said in the law of the Lord, "a pair of turtledoves, or two young pigeons." Now there was a man in Jerusalem, whose name was Simeon, and this man was righteous and devout, looking for the consolation of Israel, and the Holy Spirit was upon him. And it had been revealed to him by the Holy Spirit that he should not see death before he had seen the Lord's Christ. And inspired by the Spirit he came into the temple; and when the parents brought in the child Jesus, to do for him according to the custom of the law, he took him up in his arms and blessed God and said,

"Lord, now lettest thou thy servant depart in peace,
according to thy word;
for mine eyes have seen thy salvation
which thou hast prepared in the presence of all peoples,
a light for revelation to the Gentiles,
and for glory to thy people Israel."

And his father and his mother marveled at what was said about him; and Simeon blessed them and said to Mary his mother,

"Behold, this child is set for the fall and rising of
  many in Israel,
and for a sign that is spoken against
(and a sword will pierce through your own soul also),
that thoughts out of many hearts may be revealed."

And there was a prophetess, Anna, the daughter of Phanuel, of the tribe of Asher; she was of a great age, having lived with her husband seven years from her virginity, and as a widow till she was eighty-four. She did not depart from the temple, worshiping with fasting and prayer night and day. And coming up at that very hour she gave thanks to God, and spoke of him to all who were looking for the redemption of Jerusalem.

Behold in silence this sorrow of Our Lady.

Reflection

What if you were facing a similar prophetic word given about your life and the life of your child? How would you react? A paralyzing fear would most likely grip you—that a well-respected elder in the house of God would say such things would be deeply disturbing. Simeon fulfilled his prophetic office by being a mouthpiece for God (the Hebrew word for *prophet* means "mouth"). Like the words of every prophet in the Old Testament, Simeon's words were piercing, but unlike the words of any prophet in the Old Testament, his piercing words were strongly felt. Truly, this sword would pierce through the heart of Mary because perfect love understands that enough is never enough until it gives everything. As St. Alphonsus Liguori reminds us, "She concentrated all her love on her only Son. Nor was she afraid of going too far in loving Him. This Son was God and He deserved limitless love. This was the Son Who was at the same time the victim she was voluntarily sacrificing to death."[94]As it has been observed, "We do not grieve what we do not love." The intensity of love dictates the depth of sorrow experienced when that which is cherished is lost, endangered, mistreated, or harmed. Who could fathom the sorrows of Our Lady? She, who was "full of grace" (Lk. 1:28), was filled with a love that transcends human limitations. Consequently, her sorrow was boundless.

What is captivating about Mary's encounter with Simeon is that both she and Joseph were astonished by his words. Before this, Mary (Luke 1:26–27) and Joseph (Matthew 1:20) had their own angelic revelations regarding Jesus. Yet, they were "amazed" by Simeon's prophecy about their son. The Greek term for "amazed" suggests a continuous or progressive state. They were marveling as Simeon spoke, and then, their wonderment collided with a "sword," signifying that God's marvels are intertwined with suffering–swords that pierce the soul.

In the realm of storytelling, from myths and fables to legends and historical accounts, the sword stands as a powerful symbol of bravery and honor. It signifies strength and defense, yet it also slices through deceit and illusion. For Mary, the sword imagery foretold the deep pain and grief she would endure, particularly witnessing her Son's agony and Crucifixion. It is also a reminder that she is the queen to all those who honor her Son and go to battle against the wickedness and snares of the devil.

In Jewish symbolism, the sword also represents the tongue, wielding words that can topple men. Each hostile word directed at

[94] Liguori, *The Glories of Mary*, 411.

Christ is akin to a sword thrust into her soul, both then and now. The malicious words hurled at Christ throughout His ministry, culminating in His Crucifixion, cleave into her soul, rendering her both mourner and martyr.

Through Mary's sorrows and tears, she offers insights to those who seek to follow her path and depend on her guidance. Indeed, she imparts lessons of courage, honor, and fortitude, shielding us as she aids in revealing the falsehoods and deceits of the adversary.

What's more, Mary did not say to Simeon, "How dare you talk to me like that?" Nor did she turn her back on the prophet and walk away to put Him out of sight and out of mind. Again, Joseph and Mary "marveled" (Luke 2:33) at the words spoken by the man who was "righteous and devout" (Luke 2:25). Holiness recognizes holiness, and Joseph and Mary would have recognized the holiness of Simeon. Mary's response to the foreboding words of Simeon was a continuation of what started in the Visitation—an uncalculated offering to God of her very life, an offering that would find its climax in her sharing in her Son's suffering on Calvary. Mary's response to the angel Gabriel was an active and robust yes to God.

Those with the most extraordinary capacity for love have the most remarkable capacity for suffering. Mary's sorrow includes the division between man and God created by sin. Fr. Réginald Garrigou-Lagrange said of Our Lady, "She felt in her own heart all the physical and moral sufferings of our Lord in a measure corresponding to her love for God whom sinners offend. Just as we cannot fathom the fullness of the Holy Virgin's charity, we cannot appreciate the fullness of her sufferings."[95] As our sin breaks the

[95] Raymond Smith, O.P., and Rod Gorton, *Knowing the Love of God: Lessons from a Spiritual Master* (Dekalb, IL: Lighthouse Catholic Media, 2015), 202.

Father's heart, it is like one blow after another to the Immaculate Heart of Mary. Mary has repeatedly appeared to visionaries (in Guadalupe, Lourdes, Fátima, and Kibeho) over the centuries to urge us to return to God, and when we do, we alleviate her suffering. As Our Lady said to St. Bridget of Sweden, "I am not only mother of the just and innocent, but also sinners, provided they repent."[96] The Church's proclamation is "The kingdom of God is at hand; repent, and believe in the gospel" (Mark 1:15) not "The Kingdom of God is at hand, we welcome everyone." God's mercy is without limits—for everyone—provided they repent.

St. Dymphna and the Sorrow of Increasing Mental Illness

Simeon's prophecy that Mary would suffer was not exclusively a foretelling of the pain and suffering she would experience in the immediate future or, for that matter, in subsequent weeks or months. Instead, it was a prophecy about her whole life. As Simeon stated, the Baby he held in his arms would be the "fall and rising of many in Israel" (Luke 2:34). The entirety of Joseph and Mary's life had a shadow cast over it. As suggested in the reflection, Simeon's words would have caused great consternation for anyone and could easily have led Joseph and Mary down the path of mental anguish. For those who deal with mental health struggles, turning to Our Lady for help makes great sense. But we should also have recourse to the intercession of St. Dymphna.

St. Dymphna is the patron saint of those who struggle with mental health, anxiety, and depression. She has recently gained popularity as the world has become increasingly aware of mental health problems and their drastic effects on our daily lives. The staggering numbers of Americans grappling with depression and

[96] Liguori, *The Glories of Mary*, 46.

suicidal thoughts are at an all-time high. In fact, nearly half of young people report experiencing persistent feelings of anxiety, sadness, or hopelessness.

Mental health is important. If we neglect our mental well-being, we will suffer spiritually because we are a composite of body and soul. The Catholic Church is not an either-or but both-and. The Catholic vision of man suggests that we cannot tell where the soul ends and the body begins. The word *catholic* means "universal" or "according to the whole." Health is derived from an old English word that translates as both "wholeness" and "holiness." In fact, the most ancient translation of health translates as "holy, sacred." And this is not to be understood as just spiritual health but health as it applies to the whole human person. Why? Sin is the rupture between body and soul. The Catholic Church has long understood that the consequence of sin has a direct effect on the body: physically, emotionally, and psychologically. At its root, every psychological discussion points toward a spiritual reality.

In a report from the World Health Organization, at the turn of the third millennium, "one in four people in the world will be affected by mental or neurological disorders at some point in their lives."[97] Beyond this very high ratio is the rapid increase in mental health cases because of the anticipated long-term effects of COVID. Due to COVID, the global prevalence of anxiety and depression has increased by a massive 25 percent. Such things as fear of infection, growing financial concerns, rise in grief and bereavement from the death of loved ones, and loneliness all led to

[97] "The World Health Report 2001: Mental Disorders Affect One in Four People," World Health Organization, September 28, 2001, https://www.who.int/news-room/detail/28-09-2001-the-world-health-report-2001-mental-disorders-affect-one-in-four-people.

a spike in mental health cases.[98] In 2021 alone, there was a nearly 500 percent increase over the number of people who were screened for mental health issues in 2019 and a 103 percent increase over 2020.[99] Across the world, there are soaring levels of anxiety and an epidemic of loneliness, and these have left us with unprecedented suicide rates. In 2021, the CDC reported that 48,183 people died by suicide, estimated as one death every eleven minutes.[100] The impact of suicide extends far beyond these numbers, as many more individuals contemplate or plan suicide.

Alongside COVID, one of the contributing causes of loneliness, depression, and suicide is social media. Researchers tell us that the rise in social media in the last fifteen years is directly proportionate to the rise in mental health issues. Psychologists are in consensus that there is a tight correlation between excessive screen time and loneliness and depression (made worse by COVID-19). When we spend too much time in front of screens, we lose touch with the real world; the virtual world becomes our world, and we therefore lack needed physical community. Man is built to be in a community, not isolated from the world. We learn the language of love in our families, our neighborhoods, and our broader communities—going outside ourselves to serve others. We are created by God to be in a relationship with others—not absorbed by how others make us feel. Love is not a sentiment but an action of the heart that moves toward others. For the most part, social media is repugnant to that.

[98] Sarah D., "Mental Health America Depression Screening: Depression Talk," Depression Talk, April 5, 2024, https://www.depressiontalk.net/mental-health-america-depression-screening/.

[99] Sarah D., "Mental Health America."

[100] "Facts about Suicide," Centers for Disease Control and Prevention, last reviewed May 8, 2023, https://www.cdc.gov/suicide/facts/index.html.

What's more, in these virtual communities we create on social media, there is a great deal of negativity for the sake of negativity. What initially seemed harmless in connecting with others on social media accounts has, over time, in some cases, turned ugly with bullying and brutal attacks. The name-calling and shaming that go on in the virtual world have, for many, led to sleepless nights and, ultimately, deep sadness and depression. And how have we responded? We "unfollow" without reconciliation and create false virtual communities. We do not "love our enemies," as Jesus calls us to, but we "delete" them from our virtual spaces—this pseudo-reality we have created has impacted our social well-being because we never did, in fact, "delete" those enemies from our existence. In this context, our virtual spaces have become like an atom bomb in our families. All of this is destructive to our mental health.

Mental health is also directly impacted by divorce, broken families, bad friends, sexual trauma, and the general hedonism of our age, all of which leave terrible wounds. These wounds are often accompanied by shock, denial, bitter grievances, and feelings of being abandoned. Again, we were made for love, and this is our deepest desire. Undoubtedly, the social sciences can contribute to one's healing, but such anguish calls for the healing touch of Christ. Christ is our hope!

Mental illnesses affect many people we love, if not ourselves, and they are often very difficult to confront. The good news is that God is here to help and will respond eagerly to our prayers. So it is that we pray to St. Dymphna specifically for help and healing in this area.

Why did St. Dymphna become a special intercessor with God for those suffering from *anxiety, depression, and mental illness*?

St. Dymphna was the daughter of a divided household in seventh-century Ireland. Her mother, Odilla, a faithful Christian, was married to the Celtic king Damon, a pagan. While Odilla never converted her husband, her virtuous way left a deep impression upon young

Dymphna as she consecrated herself to Christ and took a vow of chastity at age fourteen. Unfortunately, Dymphna's mother died around this time, sending King Damon into an emotional spiral.

Damon was lost without his wife, so his advisers suggested that he remarry. Damon agreed to take a new wife only if his advisers could find someone as beautiful as his wife. The king's men searched but could find no one as beautiful as his wife except for his daughter, Dymphna. For reasons unknown, the king's men urged Damon to take Dymphna as his wife. Damon, enraged at this point, agreed and told Dymphna of his plan. Dymphna was mortified. Under the guidance of her confessor, Fr. Gerebran, Dymphna fled the country and traveled to Geel, Belgium, to hide from Damon and his court. There, along with a handful of others, including Fr. Gerebran, she ministered to the people of Geel who struggled with mental and nervous disorders.

King Damon eventually found where Dymphna and her supporters were hiding and was infuriated with them. Fr. Gerebran remained a loyal protector of Dymphna and rebuked Damon for his evil plan; this got Gerebran beheaded by Damon and his men. Damon continued to try to convince Dymphna to marry him, but his efforts were in vain. Enraged by her continued refusal, he decided the only course of action was to behead his daughter. She was only fifteen years old. Dymphna and Gerebran died as martyrs, and a church was erected where their bodies were initially buried.

As people started visiting the shrine, applying Dymphna's relic to sick patients, and praying novenas, miracles began. Because these miracles included the unexplained healing of the mentally ill, Dymphna has also been declared patron of the mentally ill. Geel, Belgium, quickly gained a world-famed reputation for caring for mentally ill and insane patients. Even today, it is considered a model community for accepting those who live with mental illness.

Like most saints, Dymphna had a difficult life, but her unwavering faith in God eternally remains an example for us all to follow and learn from. Dymphna experienced many traumas. She had to grieve her mother's death, interact with and protect herself from her mentally ill father, and learn to forgive and trust others when her life experience would have told her to do the exact opposite. She devoted her young life to serving the mentally ill. Evidently, she has continued this great work in Heaven.

As we learn from Mary how to be faithful to God's plan, we add St. Dymphna to our team of intercessors to help those who struggle with mental health issues to conform their lives to God's will.

St. Dymphna, pray for us!

Second Sorrow

THE FLIGHT INTO EGYPT

Matthew 2:13–15

Now when they had departed, behold, an angel of the Lord appeared to Joseph in a dream and said, "Rise, take the child and his mother, and flee to Egypt, and remain there till I tell you; for Herod is about to search for the child, to destroy him." And he rose and took the child and his mother by night, and departed to Egypt, and remained there until the death of Herod. This was to fulfil what the Lord had spoken by the prophet, "Out of Egypt have I called my son."

Behold in silence this sorrow of Our Lady.

Reflection

"You want me to do what! Right now?"

"Yes, we must leave right now!"

How would you react if your spouse woke you during the night and said that he or she had been told in a dream that you had to leave right now and flee to another country? Would you be angry? Confused? Maybe you would just shake your head and tell your spouse to go back to sleep. Any of these responses would be quite understandable.

But Mary's response was quite different, she simply obeyed the Lord by choosing in God's grace to follow her holy husband—this, despite the harrowing experience that awaited her.

Consider what God asked of Mary and the Holy Family. He said, "Go into a land you do not know, traveling on a road you have never seen. I know this makes no sense to you, but go, and go now!" What's more, the angel added, "remain there till I tell you." Joseph and Mary awaited God's guidance with patience and perseverance, mirroring God's own patience with them. Like the Israelites in the Old Testament, Mary experienced a period of indefinite wandering.

Before us, life's deserts stretch vast and seemingly infinite, and in our exhaustion, we call out to God. The sands shift under our feet, and we are enveloped by uncertainty. "How much longer must we wait, God?" Our hearts ache with this plea. We yearn for answers, for relief, for a glimpse of the oasis on the horizon. Yet, like Mary, we learn to trust even when the path is obscured.

Joseph and Mary's ongoing conversation with God was underscored by the grim reality that "Herod is about to search for the child, to destroy him." For a search to be genuinely human, it must culminate in a definitive end. This inescapable truth casts a shadow over the entire story; Herod is determined to achieve one objective: the assassination of the newborn King!

There were two roads to Egypt. Mary and Joseph would have avoided the shorter and easier one to decrease the chances of their being seen. The road less traveled for the Holy Family would have been a little over two hundred miles. Joseph and Mary rose up with one thing in mind: do as the Father asks![101] The Holy Family's flight

[101] Incidentally, God asked the same thing of Abraham when he told him, "Go from your country and your kindred and your father's

probably included a great deal of physical suffering and the alarm of being overtaken at any moment by a detachment of soldiers. In the end, through Mary's obedience—with all the dangers before her and the Holy Family—God's desired end worked out and was eventually understood.

The flight into Egypt reminds us that obedience saves. This can be hard for our contemporary ears to hear. Today, rebellion against law, order, and the natural structure of life is encouraged, and obedience is despised. Saying no to authority figures and being a rebel are lionized in our culture. In this context, the world opposes God. Yet obedience is being not childish but childlike, listening to the voice of God with the utmost faith that there is no self-interestedness in God but the single interest that we are saved in His love.

In the narrative of the Flight into Egypt, we are reminded that Mary could have reacted far differently to Joseph and his dream, but she did not. Again, Mary faced the world's first attempt to take her Son's life—not merely rejection, but an actual threat to His existence; a foreshadowing of what was to come at Calvary. Such sorrow could have crushed her heart, yet her love for God moved her to respond. She drew from her interior attitude of faith and listened carefully to the Holy Spirit, and the Holy Spirit carried her up and over the raging waters that were trying to overtake her and her Son. Mary's heart speaks, "I am certain it will be okay—though I'm uncertain of what 'okay' entails or looks like, God assured it will be okay, and so it shall be." Indeed, trust and Obedience are intertwined expressions of faith and acceptance. They demonstrate our reliance on God's love, even when outcomes are uncertain.

---

house to a land that I will show you" (Gen. 12:1), and Abraham did go, as we hear in Hebrews 11:8: "He went out, not knowing where he was to go" (11:8).

May we learn from Mary's example and be better listeners to the Spirit, obeying the Word of God, even if what God asks from us appears daunting. Mary's sorrows are synonymous with the daunting—if we live in the daunting, we will be close to her.

St. Joseph and the Sorrow of the Broken Family

The story of the Flight into Egypt has multiple layers and more than one star character. Still, it is arguably the humble carpenter from Nazareth, St. Joseph, who stands as the chief protagonist of this narrative about the Holy Family. And where there is a protagonist, there is always a villain.

The villain is Herod—the archetype of all villains, as he sought to kill the God-Man, Jesus Christ. Satan, speaking and acting through Herod, set out to destroy the Holy Family; Joseph, the guardian of the Holy Family, protected Jesus and Mary from the snares of the devil.

St. Joseph was an ordinary man with great faith in and obedience to God, and God relied on him to do great things. In the flight into Egypt, St. Joseph did what God wanted him to do, and he did it promptly and wholeheartedly, without wavering or faltering, even though it meant complicating his life, going to a country whose customs, people, and language were unknown to him. With Mary by his side, he did whatever was necessary to protect his family, God's family, against Satan. For this reason, in a day and age when we are witnessing an unprecedented attack on the family—an attack that grieves the heart of Mary—we turn to St. Joseph, the patron of families. Indeed, it brings Mary great joy when we seek the intercession of her beloved husband.

Sr. Lucia dos Santos, one of the three children who witnessed the Marian apparitions in Fátima in 1917, predicted that the final battle between Christ and Satan would be over marriage and the family. As previously discussed, there is an interweaving between Our Lady of Sorrows and Our Lady of Fátima.

The message of Our Lady of Fátima should come as no surprise to any of us. Satan's greatest scheme has as its end goal to destroy the family. Why? Because the family is at the heart of our culture. If you strike at the family, you pierce society. In the words of St. John Paul II, "The family is the first and vital cell of society."[102]

Marx once declared, "Abolish the family!" In this statement, he was employing Satan's strategy to bring more chaos to the world. Holy Mother Church says that the family is the headwaters of every social institution, and she means what she says. The Judeo-Christian understanding of family is as the cell of society because loving families produce children that benefit society: hard workers, just employers, business owners with a moral compass, statesmen and politicians who lead and govern with integrity, and so on.

God has entrusted to all parents a particular mission and responsibility: to be at the service of the world. God is love, and the degree to which we enter the mystery of that love—willing the good of our spouses and children—is the measure that we transform society. The praying family opens itself up to the most profound language of God, the language that surrenders itself for others with no expectation of receiving anything in return. The family that prays and loves in the home is the family that transforms everything outside the home. If families are not working to transform the world, the world will transform the family.

The praying and loving family is the intact family, and intact families keep their members out of trouble. Gang members rarely

[102] Pope John Paul II, apostolic exhortation on the Role of the Christian Family in the Modern World *Familiaris Consortio* (November 22, 1981), no. 42.

come from intact families, and an estimated 80 percent of all crime is gang related. What would our society look like if we were a culture of intact families living with low poverty and low crime? It would be a moral and just society. Destroy the family, and it will leave a trail of destruction in its path. This can be seen in:

- Increasing divorce rates
- Mainstream pornography (more on this later)
- Record high drug and alcohol abuse
- Climbing prostitution
- The murder of unborn children
- The growing number of movies and television shows presenting fathers and the traditional family in a negative light
- The widespread acceptance of gender ideology

Friends, when we begin to tap into the indicators of what is wrong with culture, we ought to be reminded to "be sober; be watchful" (1 Pet. 5:8); the attack is ubiquitous—an evil smoke that goes unnoticed, slipping under our doors, penetrating everything, everywhere.

That being said, it is one thing to identify the consequences and another to do something about it. What are we doing about this seemingly impossible task of reclaiming our families to reclaim the world? God leads with mercy, and so should we.

If you are in a broken relationship, seek to forgive and reconcile. If you cannot forgive yourself for something you have done, go to Confession and begin the work of healing. Allow God into those places in your heart that have been neglected, and let Jesus claim them; only Jesus knows the full extent of our hearts' desires, and the Lover of souls desires that you be set free. The more attention you give to reconciliation, the better off your family will be—and that includes your extended family, neighborhood, parish community, and so on. Do you want to change the world? Let God love you into freedom; the rest will take care of itself.

St. Joseph knew a thing about unreservedly letting God into his heart and living as a guardian of the Holy Family. We turn to him in our hour of need to be better intercessors for a world that needs the family in order to rediscover its identity in Christ.

St. Joseph was a just man who worked as a carpenter in the silence of Nazareth. *Silence*, *carpenter*, *just*: each of these words is a preeminent truth from Sacred Scripture that teaches us something about St. Joseph and, hopefully, ourselves.

Consider this: although St. Joseph is such a powerful saint, we do not have a single recorded word of his. Did St. Joseph talk to Jesus and Mary? Of course he did, but if silence speaks, St. Joseph shows us how. Where you might find the phrase "action speaks louder than words," you ought to find a picture of St. Joseph.

Much of what we know about St. Joseph is tied to the place of deepest silence: sleep. Three times, an angel of God appeared to St. Joseph in a dream and told him what to do: take Mary as your wife; flee to Egypt; return to Israel. Each time, without reservation, St. Joseph responded. Out of silence, Joseph moved and lived in God. If the family ever recovers its moral compass, it will learn from the great St. Joseph. In the words of Pope Benedict XVI, "Let us allow ourselves to be filled with St. Joseph's silence! In a world that is often too noisy, that encourages neither recollection nor listening to God's voice, we are in such deep need of it."[103] Indeed, the noise of the world and all of its empty promises call for every one of us to consider the genius of St. Joseph's silence.

The silence of St. Joseph is reflected in the Holy Family. In quiet obedience, Jesus grew "in wisdom and in stature" (Luke 2:51–52).

[103] Pope Benedict XVI, Angelus, December 18, 2005.

Think about it. God was obedient to man—specifically, to a very holy man! And not for a short period, but 91 percent of His time on earth. Maybe we don't think of it because there is so little we know about it besides its hidden nature. There was no social media, but He would have condemned its noise even if there were. Nazareth was tucked away in a cup of hills, removed from the clamor of the busy roads and commercialism in Israel. Silence speaks.

What little we know of St. Joseph teaches us something about the man whose intercession we seek. Joseph was a carpenter. The Greek word for carpenter is *tekton*, which had various meanings in the ancient world. Generally speaking, *tektons* were highly skilled laborers who were adept at all kinds of handiwork. A *tekton* could be a simple carpenter or a master craftsman working in either wood or masonry. In the ancient world, a *tekton* was the person each village depended on to help build their homes, fix doors, and so on. It could be said that Joseph was the "handyman" of the village. Every family and neighborhood had a handyman; Nazareth had theirs. It is no wonder everyone knew Jesus as "the carpenter's son" (Matt. 13:55). Sometimes, the "carpenter" may have laid the foundation for their homes or built their fireplaces.

The God-Man's foster father offered God his daily duties, and in that offering, his work was sanctified and redeemed. We can be assured of this because Joseph was a "just man" (Matt. 1:19).

What does this word *just* mean in its original biblical context? To be just was to be obedient to the law of Israel as it would have been received in the first century, notably in the first five books of the Bible, the Pentateuch. The just man was a strict observer of the laws of Moses and one who walked in the integrity of God (see Prov. 20:7). The just man, then, was a man whose whole life was formed by the law of God, the revealed truths of God; he was attuned to the ways of God and lived in God according to those ways. It could be said that the just man was the man who set his heart on the law of God in such a profound way that its beat was to the rhythm of that law. In the Old Testament, the law of God included the heart of God. St. Joseph's heart was synchronized with the heart of God, as he was a man of moral character, living uprightly in all his days. The Greek word for *just* is *diakois*, meaning "having reached its end, finished, complete." In doing God's will in his daily life, St. Joseph lived out the purpose, or end, for which he was created. Much of this "living out" was in the home.

St. Joseph holds many titles in the life of the Church, including "Glory of Domestic Life." Many of us look upon domestic life as humdrum. How many of us have wondered why we spend so much time fixing pipes, mopping floors, or doing laundry? The life of St. Joseph is a reminder that nothing goes to waste; not a single action is lost on God. Indeed, St. Joseph's life was "a holy and acceptable" offering to God (see Rom. 12:1–3). For this reason, he is the Glory of Domestic Life!

The family of the twenty-first century needs to pay close attention to St. Joseph, who was silent and just in the quiet space of Nazareth, where he embraced the ordinary, showing us what it takes to be a saint. Whether you are a carpenter, an electrician, a teacher, a homemaker, or an accountant—St. Joseph can remind you that God calls you to give Him your days so that what you do will become the saintly work it was intended to be.

Dear readers, on the one hand, the world will not stop persecuting the family as long as the world follows the ways of the devil. Still, families in the world can be won over by the family that embraces its primary vocation to pray, love, and work in the home as Jesus, Mary, and Joseph did, in silence.

Undoubtedly, St. Joseph concentrated on building and nurturing his family with a fierce determination, for he understood the enemy's attacks and how they were ever present and relentless. St. Joseph is the Terror of Demons (another one of his titles) because he countered Satan's chaotic, busy noise with a heroic, simple silence.

St. Joseph, pray for us!

Third Sorrow

THE LOSS OF THE CHILD JESUS IN THE TEMPLE

Luke 2:41–51

Now his parents went to Jerusalem every year at the feast of the Passover. And when he was twelve years old, they went up according to custom; and when the feast was ended, as they were returning, the boy Jesus stayed behind in Jerusalem. His parents did not know it, but supposing him to be in the company they went a day's journey, and they sought him among their kinsfolk and acquaintances; and when they did not find him, they returned to Jerusalem, seeking him. After three days they found him in the temple, sitting among the teachers, listening to them and asking them questions; and all who heard him were amazed at his understanding and his answers. And when they saw him they were astonished; and his mother said to him, "Son, why have you treated us so? Behold, your father and I have been looking for you anxiously." And he said to them, "How is it that you sought me? Did you not know that I must be in my Father's house?" And they did not understand the saying which he spoke to them. And he went down with them and came to Nazareth, and was obedient to them; and his mother kept all these things in her heart.

Behold in silence this sorrow of Our Lady.

Reflection

Anyone who has experienced losing sight of his or her child at a mall or an amusement park knows the sudden and paralyzing fear that grips a person in that moment. You cannot do or even think about anything else until you find your child. Everything else is put on hold—everything! The possibility of losing a child is a parent's worst fear.

Mary and Joseph did not have the benefit of calling 911, having the authorities issue an Amber Alert, or filing a missing-person report. They lived through three days of having to search for Jesus. They looked everywhere, for seventy-two long hours, but did not find Jesus. It has been said that when you lose something close to you, the brain gets so fixated on the loss that the brain's chemistry communicates time differently: minutes turn into hours, hours into days, days into weeks, and so on. Again, seventy-two long hours. They searched everywhere—every place where Jesus "should have been"—but He was nowhere to be found.

It might seem odd that they could have lost Jesus so completely in the first place. But given the cultural context, it's very understandable that the Holy Family would not have necessarily noticed Jesus' absence as they would not have been walking home in each other's company. Jewish men and young boys near Bar-Mitzvah age would walk together, while the women and girls would walk in large familial groups toward the front. It was only after a time, after leaving Jerusalem to head home, that Joseph and Mary noticed Jesus missing from the group of young Jewish boys he was spending time with. It was then that they experienced the profound emptiness and sorrow of losing their Son.

For Mary, her three-day sorrow would anticipate the darkness that overshadowed her during the Passover of the Cross—Christ's descent into Hell and the preaching of the good news to the just who had gone before Him.[104] Mary's third sorrow was not distant from the first sorrow. In the first sorrow, Simeon told her that a sword would pierce her heart. Was she pondering these words as a "sword" that would pierce her heart? As previously discussed, because we know from Scripture that Mary pondered all things in her heart and that God revealed things to her over time, we can extract that she had certain spiritual sensitivities and wisdom that were much greater than ours.

But what are we to make of Mary's anxiety? This is a crucial question. Not only were Mary and Joseph searching for Jesus "anxiously," but Luke also urges us to "behold" this truth (Luke 2:48).

Mary was anxious, yet her response was an ordered response because her emotions were perfectly aligned with her reason. In contrast, our anxiety is frequently chaotic, as our flawed nature tends to intensify it, leading to irrational behavior. Mary's anxiety was due to the loss of her Son—a rational reaction to the circumstances. Mary's anxious search for Jesus was not marked by an absence of faith but was imbued with faith. Mary was passing through the dark night of the soul. In this faith-filled darkness, a soul advances toward unity with God. It is a period in which God may appear remote, silent, and concealed. This darkness is not without meaning, however; it acts as a forge for spiritual development and cleansing; in such darkness, God reveals intimate secrets,

[104] See Pope Benedict XVI, *Jesus of Nazareth, The Infancy Narratives* (San Francisco: Ignatius Press, 2012), 123.

because in darkness is when lovers are most intimate. For Mary, the finding of Jesus in the temple was a journey of profound intimacy.

A key point emerges from a deeper analysis of the Greek term for "anxious." The word used here is *odynōmenoi*, which translates as "causing intense pain; anguish or agony, being tormented; suffering." This Greek term appears only one other time in Sacred Scripture, in Acts 20:38, where the Ephesian elders are "sorrowing" (*odynōmenoi*) because they know they will never see Paul's face again. They are not merely "anxious" about his leaving; they feel intense pain, a sort of agony due to his anticipated absence. With this in mind, let's revisit the words of Luke 2:48 with this revision. "Behold, Your father and I have been sorrowing in our search for You." Mary was "sorrowing" because Jesus was absent from her. She was in profound "anguish"—tormented by the reality of not seeing the face of her growing Boy. Likewise, all of Mary's sorrows are encapsulated in this singular truth—the soul that does not see the face of Jesus. Indeed, we are called to "behold" the "sorrowing" Mother, and we do this when we recite the Chaplet of the Seven Sorrows of Mary.

We all go through sorrows in life. How have our past sorrows prepared us for possible greater sorrows in the future as they cause us to lean even closer to our Heavenly Father? When stress and anxiety try to paralyze us, contemplating and praying the Seven Sorrows Chaplet keeps us open to being recipients of God's grace. We become receivers rather than dispensers of charity. Receptivity always precedes dispensation. In this case, the receiving is the grace of understanding how God is conforming our hearts to the Immaculate Heart of Mary and the Sacred Heart of Jesus, however long it takes. Again, Mary has much to teach us here. Even her incomparable faith was a " 'journeying' faith, a faith that is repeatedly shrouded in darkness and maturing by persevering through the darkness. Mary does not understand Jesus' saying [that He had to be in His Father's house], but she keeps it in her heart and allows it gradually to come to maturity there."[105] Mary says to us: Let me teach you how to understand and ponder.

Jesus, even when seemingly lost or hidden, was always about His Father's work. His Crucifixion appeared dark, yet it led to resurrection. In your own struggles, remember that God is at work—even when clarity eludes you. Trust that each step draws you closer to Him.

One last note: notice *where* Mary found Jesus—in the Temple. Every adoration chapel is a "new temple" where God waits for you. You will find Him there waiting for you. Jesus is physically present in your local adoration chapel, waiting to preach to your heart. He will leave you "amazed" as He answers the deepest questions of your heart (see Luke 2:47).

St. Jospehine Bakhita and the Sorrow of Human Trafficking

In today's world, an even greater evil can accompany losing a child or a loved one. The sheer number of missing, trafficked children and adults is increasing at a frightening rate. The fear that accompanies even the idea of this happening to a loved one—especially a child—is truly chilling.

The story of St. Josephine Bakhita sings of a hope that transcends the fear of losing a loved one to the insidious crime of human trafficking. Our sister St. Josephine bore the scars of her abduction, slavery, and abuse both internally and externally. No one ever forgets that kind of torture and abuse. But what she did with that memory is crucial for us to see. She chose gratitude over

[105] Pope Benedict XVI, *Jesus of Nazareth*, 125.

resentment and hatred, the little way of love and service to Christ over bitterness and anger. She took the opportunity that was given to her to speak up and seek her freedom and then to use that freedom to learn more about God and Our Lady. St. Josephine Bakhita is a beacon of light shining over an ocean of despair and vulnerability of the worst kind, that of children and young people who are trafficked and sold.

In 2023, the movie *Sound of Freedom*, starring Jim Caviezel, reminded us that the problem of human trafficking has gotten exponentially worse in recent years. The worldwide atrocity of human trafficking has swollen to a $150 billion-a-year business. Why such growth? Among the many accurate details that Jim Caviezel brought to the screen was the simple fact that many cartels are moving from the drug industry to human trafficking because cocaine can be sold once, but a child can be sold five or six times a day for sometimes as long as ten years. This truth ought to rip out our hearts! There are more humans trapped in slavery today than at any other time in history. Millions of these enslaved people are children.

The loss of a child to sex trafficking is incomprehensible. The structures in place to advance the sickness of human traffickers are far beyond imagination, just as the evil both surrounding and enabling it at different levels is truly grave. We wonder: "If God is so loving, why are there evils in the world like human trafficking?"

The answer actually lies within the question. Because God is love, there is evil in the world. Love never coerces. It can never be forced. There is evil in the world because free will is necessary for love. The moment anyone forces love, it ceases to be love. The ultimate cause of the despicable evil of human trafficking is not God but sin—sin committed by people driven by lust, money, and power. Sin reduces us to animals who treat others like animals.

Men are made to be loved and things are made to be used, but, instead, we use people and love things. God will not control any person; each of our actions is done according to our own free will. People give their lusts and desire free reign, and this means that the innocent often suffer. When people succumb to their sense appetites, being controlled by Satan, they make it painfully obvious how immeasurably evil and destructive sin is.

We can be sure that God is heartbroken by the sin of human trafficking. He would like nothing more than to reach out His hand and make it all right. Moreover, when God's heart is broken, so is Mary's; when God wants to intervene, so does Mary. As we grieve with Mary over the misery of the loss of innocence of millions of children, we do so as intercessors of faith. Never lose sight that as our prayers mingle with the incense that is the prayer of the saints (see Rev. 8:4), God unleashes that prayer upon the world, and it brings to fruition what is the will of God. God has desired ends and invites us to be the means to help achieve those ends. The more we grieve with the heart of Mary, the deeper our desire grows to pray for what grieves her heart. Let us be intercessors with Mary, and grace will be unleashed upon the world.

There are 7.9 billion people in the world, 2.2 billion of whom are children. God has the deepest love for each one, and His heart bleeds to see them suffer. He wants to see each one prosper and flourish (see Jer. 29:11). Jesus reminds us that the very hairs on each of our heads are numbered (see Matt. 10:30). The hairs on our heads are not more closely monitored than those on the head of a ten-year-old snatched away into captivity.

Many of us have been born into a place of love and safety. Maybe some of us feel guilty when we see the suffering of the innocent. We shouldn't feel guilty, but we should feel compelled, at the very least, to pray and to offer to God our little and big sufferings for the big suffering that is the loss of innocence of little ones.

Josephine Bakhita was born in 1869 in a small village in the Darfur region of Sudan. At the age of seven, she was kidnapped while working in the fields with her family. She was sold and resold into slavery five times. When Josephine's initial captors asked for her name, she was so terrified that she couldn't answer, so her captors named her Bakhita, which means "fortunate" in Arabic. In a God-like twist, this would prove to be providential.

The first years of her life looked nothing like that of a girl who was "fortunate." Her early years were filled with torture. Josephine was beaten, cut, and branded by her various owners. Her biography noted one terrifying moment when her master cut her 114 times and poured salt in her wounds to ensure that the scars remained. She remarked, "I felt I was going to die any moment, especially when they rubbed me in with the salt."[106] Remarkably, she persevered.

The fifth time she was sold, Bakhita was purchased by Callisto Legnani, the Italian consul in Khartoum, the capital of Sudan. Two years later, he took Bakhita to Italy to work as a nanny for his colleague, Augusto Michieli. This move was the "fortunate" moment in the life of young Bakhita.

Michieli sent Bakhita to accompany his daughter to a school in Venice run by the Canossian Sisters. There, as she listened to the teachings of the Canossian Sisters, young Bakhita fell in love with the teachings of the Church and desired to become Catholic. In 1890, she received the Sacraments of Initiation and took the name Josephine Margaret. Josephine means "God will increase," and Margaret, "pearl."

[106] Roberto Zanini, *Bakhita: From Slave to Saint* (San Francisco: Ignatius Press, 2013), 63.

In the meantime, Michieli wanted to take Josephine and his daughter back to Sudan, but Josephine refused to return. The disagreement escalated and was taken to the Italian courts, where it was ruled that Josephine could stay in Italy, where slavery was not recognized and thus, Josephine was a free woman. She remained in Italy and decided to enter the Canossians in 1893. In 1896, Josephine Margaret Bakhita made her final vows in the Canossian Order at age twenty-nine. She was sent to Northern Italy, where she dedicated her life to assisting her community and teaching others to love God.

Toward the end of her life, in an astounding moment of God-like love and forgiveness, she said, "If I were to meet the slave traders who kidnapped me and even those who tortured me, I would kneel and kiss their hands, for if that did not happen, I would not be a Christian and Religious today."[107] Josephine died in 1947 at the age of seventy-eight. Indeed, she was a woman who found great fortune, a pearl that never lost her value, and as she followed God, God used her to increase His Kingdom!

Josephine was beatified in 1992 and canonized in October 2000 by Pope John Paul II. Her canonization was one of the first of the third millennium—a clear message from God that we need her intercession for this millennium in which we are seeing the skyrocketing of human trafficking.

Dear readers, it is evident that St. Josephine Bakhita refused to accept a victim mentality, even though she would have every reason to accept being a victim. Her life shows us that forgiveness liberates us from the tyranny of memories and our endless tendency to relive hurts, pains, and all the injustices we experience. We just don't let them go, but instead, we turn them over as sacrificial gifts to the Sorrowful Heart of Mary.

[107] Zanini, *Bakhita*, 98.

How St. Josephine accepted the events that determined the direction of her life is nothing short of heroic, but, as she would remind us, this was possible only by the grace of God. Josephine forgave those who harmed her; in this, she imitated our sorrowful Mother, who also rejected a victim identity by embracing what God asked of her. St. Josephine was often seen wearing a medal of Our Lady of Sorrows. We can be confident that she united her sorrow to Our Lady's, and such union brought her immense relief and eventual joy.

Before Josephine outwardly chose to forgive her assailants, she inwardly chose Jesus and Mary. Her faith, hope, and love were virtuously manifested in her words of forgiveness: "I would kneel and kiss their hands."

We might say, "Well, I could not do that if it happened to me." St. Josephine would probably agree, but that's the whole point: with man, very little is possible; with God, everything is possible. As St. Paul says, "I can do all things in him who strengthens me" (Phil. 4:13).

St. Josephine, pray for us!

Fourth Sorrow

THE MEETING OF JESUS AND MARY ON THE WAY TO CALVARY

Luke 23:27

And there followed him a great multitude of the people, and of women who bewailed and lamented him.

Behold in silence this sorrow of Our Lady.

Reflection

For thirty years in Nazareth, Mary lovingly observed her Son. She witnessed His sleeping, eating, playing, praying, and learning from her most virtuous husband, Joseph. Then, for an additional three years, she saw her Son preach, teach, heal, cast out demons, and perform miracles. The masses went to extraordinary lengths to follow Him; they shouted out to Him in admiration, loved Him, and adored Him! His thirty-three years led to a triumphant entry into Jerusalem on Palm Sunday, where He was welcomed as a king. As Mary gazed upon her Son, the King, she would have felt pride, like any mother, admiring the magnitude of Jesus' achievements. Yet she had already endured three swords to her heart, and she was aware that more was to come.

Humans are fickle, a trait that is starkly evident in the days following Palm Sunday, when adulation shifts to betrayal and affection to animosity. Mary now witnesses her Son in agony, rejected, and with very few by His side. The Via Dolorosa (the Way of the Cross) has begun. The journey of approximately 0.4 miles from Antonia Fortress to Calvary is in motion.

Mary, determined to be by the side of her Son—condemned as a criminal—in His gravest hour, braved the danger of a hostile crowd. Strengthened by faith and courage, her heroic love remained steadfast. She aimed to stay as near to Jesus as divine providence permitted.

Jesus is now mutilated, battered, and bloodstained. As Mary watches, the once cherished recollections of Nazareth are being overshadowed by the grim journey of the Via Dolorosa. Every maternal instinct within her yearns to reach out to Jesus, to embrace Him, and to protect Him from further harm, offering solace and comfort. Yet she understands that Jesus is destined to renew all things, and this renewal is intertwined with the divine "must" of Calvary. In her heart, she draws near to Jesus, knowing that a face-to-face encounter will suffice, for every face-to-face interaction with Jesus is "the enough" amid one's suffering.

Beauty has experienced an irreversible transformation; it must tread the path of the Cross, for the ascent to Heaven is marked not by ease and privilege but by trials and tribulations. The profound paradox of our Faith is that the Cross has become the emblem of beauty, as Heaven's grand claim is that beauty, indeed, killed the beast. Thus, we pursue the Way of the Cross with Mary if we wish to kill the beast in our own lives.

In early Christianity, "the Way" was a term used to encapsulate the essence of the Christian faith; it is a phrase that predates *Christian*. "The Way," a recurrent phrase in the New Testament, underscored the reality that Christianity was a set of beliefs that formed and informed a way of life, a path walked in the footsteps of Jesus—the footsteps of discipleship and profound change—the Way of the Cross, the way of love.

Love inspires love, and has the history of man ever witnessed such mutually inspired love than when the eyes of Jesus and Mary met on the way to Golgotha? Have two humans ever held each other's gaze as Jesus and Mary did two thousand years ago? Mary sees the torn flesh of Jesus, and her heart is fractured, but as she looks into her Son's reddened eyes, she encounters the greatest love, the love that makes all things new in the Cross. The eyes of Jesus were not only red from weariness and blood, but as Revelation reminds us, they "were like flames of fire" (Rev. 1:14). Robert Frost says that the eyes are like windows into the soul. Mary looks into her Son's eyes, and they speak: "Although draped in blood, the red you see, mother, is the fire of love set ablaze for the salvation of souls. Come with me to the top of the mountain and share in my victory." In that moment in history that bore witness to the heights of all kinds of contrasting emotion—screaming, jeering, crying and wailing—there was another contrast: the most intense gaze of love against the backdrop of the most intense hate.

Bl. Pier Giorgio Frassati and the Sorrow of Youth Losing Their Identity

In Mary, we see ourselves present to our loved ones in their most dire places. Through Mary, we are encouraged to accompany the souls entrusted to us.

Most of us know at least one youth—maybe our own child, a grandchild, a niece or nephew, or a friend—who has lost his or her way. What causes young people to lose their way? Many things, some of which have already been discussed in this book, but there is one thing at its center: the love that binds people together has been lost. The loss of faith, broken families, drug and alcohol abuse, illicit sex, prostitution, the occult, gangs, and suicide—all of these tragedies have one thing in common: *the absence of love.* The overarching truth that our youth are being lost leaves a hole in Mary's heart. We must lift our hearts, full of love, and pray to Mary. Mary calls us to be at her side, praying feverishly with her and to her, drawing the youth back to her heart. In doing this, we ask the great Bl. Pier Giorgio Frassati, patron saint of youth, to accompany our prayer.

At the beginning of John Paul II's World Youth Days, he chose Bl. Frassati to be the patron of the annual events held across the globe. Since then, Bl. Frassati has found a special place in the hearts of many youth worldwide. Young Pier Giorgio was a man with whom youth can identify. He lived an ordinary life with an extraordinary heart—a man of the outdoors who loved to engage in holy conversation with the community that God surrounded him with. He was a man of encounter, seeing Christ in all things and in a particular way through the community of the Church and the Holy Eucharist. He was a man who received and shared the love of God. As we lift our eyes to Mary and seek to accompany her in prayer and help the youth in our circle, let us invite Bl. Frassati into this beautiful conversation of prayer.

What is underneath Generation Z's unprecedented identity crisis? We reached out to youth ministers, young adult leaders, and priests to ask what they see as the biggest problem facing Generation Z—those born in the late 1990s and early 2000s. As these ministers and leaders see it, for the large majority of these young people, the biggest problem is not drugs, alcohol, pornography, or gangs but an identity crisis—the consequence of the absence of love. Let us be clear: drugs, alcohol, pornography, and gangs are all grave problems and bring extraordinary grief to Our Lady, but what is at the center of this grief? Identity theft. And we are not talking about credit cards and loan numbers but the more important reality that youth are not becoming who God is calling them to be; and the tragedy of that beauty lost—the beauty that is the fullness of God alive in every teenager—is a profound sorrow to Our Lady!

With the influx of information at our fingertips, an increasing number of Generation Z are turning to their smartphones for answers to the deepest questions about life. Do a Google search, and you will find headlines such as "look inward and explore," "discover yourself," "do things that make you happy," and "ignore judgment." In short, focus entirely on yourself. What is the grave misfortune of such a focus? When we reduce our identity exclusively to what we think, our emotion gets the ruling vote, and every objective standard is lost. All we have to do is click "thumbs down" or "not like," and we do not have to debate essential truths. Those in Generation Z are building a wall around themselves, and what they are keeping out is reality, the reality of hard truths that challenge them to be who God is calling them to be (and we can also say this includes all of us, to some degree). Is it any wonder that teens are questioning who they are and turning to drugs, alcohol, and sex to try to satisfy the deepest longings of their hearts?

There are a lot of podcasts, books, and YouTube teachings out there about "who God says we are," but if they leave out who God is, it leaves the most important person out of the love equation. Members of Generation Z are living in a world that has shoved God to the margins, and even in Christian circles, we have stopped asking the right question about God: "Who is God?" What do statements such as "God loves you" and "God has chosen you" mean to a broken teenager who does not know God and has experienced only the absence of love?

So what are we to do?

We begin to bring who God is into their life by bringing the paschal love of the Cross into every encounter we have with Generation Z. We don't shrink back from walking with them but accompany them into who God is calling them to be by bringing into their lived experience the God who forgives, heals, restores, calls, and sustains. We meet them where they are and draw them into opportunities to encounter God in radical and life-changing ways, such as retreats, conferences, spiritual-formation opportunities at the local parish level, and so on. We get them to ask the first question asked in the New Testament, the question asked by the Magi: "Where is He?" And, as they experience transformation and pursue God with a steadfast heart, the holes in their hearts will be filled with purpose and meaning, filling Our Lady's heart with joy!

The reason for today's identity crisis is that we have rejected the God who created us and loves us as a Father. Cut off from the source of all life and truth, we clutch and grasp at things that leave us empty. If history has taught us anything, it is that humanity will sink into confusion, despair, and reckless violence without the knowledge of God and the saving blood of Jesus that flows from His side in the sacramental Church.

The saints are real men and women who claimed their identity in Christ. They became who they were intended to be not because they bought the latest self-help book at the local bookstore but because they went to the local chapel to better understand who God is. Among the litany of young saints, as noted above, let us turn to the young Italian Pier Giorgio Frassati to assist us in our intercessory prayer for Generation Z.

Pier Giorgio Frassati was born to an upper-middle-class family in Turin, Italy, on April 6, 1901. His father, Alfredo Frassati, editor of the popular newspaper *La Stampa*, was an agnostic. Pier Giorgio's mother, Adelaide, was a painter. Pier Giorgio's parents were not very complimentary of him, often accusing him of lacking a taste for the good things in life and even, at times, offering disparaging words about his slow intellect. One particular moment in Pier Giorgio's young adolescence would prove to have a significant impact on him. As a child, he answered the door of their home and found a mother and her child begging. His heart swelled with love, and he took off his shoes and gave them to the shoeless child. This would be the first of thousands of acts of charity in the young saint's life.

In 1913, Pier Giorgio failed his exams and was sent to a Jesuit school, where the thirteen-year-old led a vibrant spiritual life, often wanting to talk about his love for the Blessed Virgin and Jesus in the Blessed Sacrament. He joined the Apostleship of Prayer group and the Most Holy Sacrament apostolate. These Catholic groups proved essential to Pier Giorgio, steering his life toward sanctity and holiness. His high school days were punctuated by morning and evening prayer, and everything in between was filled with charity and holy recreation, including mountain climbing with fellow members of these groups.

In 1918, at age seventeen, Pier Giorgio passed his exams and entered the Royal Polytechnic University to study to be an engineer. While at the school, he joined the St. Vincent de Paul Conference to help poor soldiers after the war. With the intent to go deeper in his relationship with Mary, Pier joined the Militias of Mary and became a member of the Dominican Third Order. During this time, he continued his passion—mountain climbing with his friends—but he did not cease to help the poor, the homeless, and the sick. He often assisted the demobilized servicemen returning from World War I and those in need during the Spanish flu epidemic. It is believed that he contracted polio during one of his visits to the slums of Turin.

On Tuesday, June 30, 1925, Pier Giorgio experienced severe pain in his back muscles during a walk with two friends. Upon his return home, he felt a violent headache. Two days later, a doctor found that his reflexes no longer worked, and he was diagnosed with acute infectious polio. Pier Giorgio then went through great suffering, which he offered to Jesus. In his last days, while bedridden, the heroic saint shared the names of people who still needed assistance in the slums of Turin. A saint's heart always beats for the poor until the last breath.

On July 4, 1925, Pier Giorgio Frassati received the last rites. Then paralysis gradually spread to his lungs. After much pain, Pier Giorgio died surrounded by his family in prayer, saying, "Let me die in peace, in your holy company."

Pier Giorgio was a man who constantly desired holy company because he had always found his identity in God. Like most young men, he could have been discouraged by the many disparaging remarks made by his parents, but the Spirit of God filled his heart with the life-giving power of joy and a deep sense of encountering God everywhere and in everyone. He did not succumb to the rampant identity theft of Satan; instead, he encountered God in the Blessed Sacrament every day and was a man of the Rosary.

He also met God in nature, seeing the mountains of Turin as a kind of natural cathedral. As an accomplished mountain climber, he would understand the many parallels between Catholic life and his favorite pastime. He regularly organized trips into the mountains with occasions for prayers and holy conversations on the way up to or down from the summit. In his final climb, he wrote a short note on a photograph: *Verso L'Alto,* which means "To the Heights." This phrase has become both his epitaph and a motto for those inspired by him.

Young Pier Giorgio was a man who had a heart for accompaniment; whether it was consoling those dying from the Spanish flu epidemic, helping other young men understand who they were in God, or in the many holy conversations that made all his company with others holy, he saw the need to accompany others into becoming who God made them to be.

Bl. Pier Giorgio Frassati, pray for us!

Fifth Sorrow

THE CRUCIFIXION

John 19:25–27

Standing by the cross of Jesus were his mother, and his mother's sister, Mary the wife of Clopas, and Mary Magdalene. When Jesus saw his mother, and the disciple whom he loved standing near, he said to his mother, "Woman, behold, your son!" Then he said to the disciple, "Behold, your mother!" And from that hour the disciple took her to his own home.

Behold in silence this sorrow of Our Lady.

Reflection

What was going through the mind of Mary as she watched her Son slowly die on the Cross? What passed through the heart of our suffering Mother? What was she made to remember?

Memory is one of the greatest and most mysterious powers of the human spirit. Everything seen, heard, and done from early childhood is conserved in this immense womb, ready to reawaken and to dance into the light either by an external stimulus or by our own will. The scent of rain on warm earth, the lullabies whispered by a grandmother, the taste of salt on ocean breezes—they linger, waiting for their cue to reawaken.

I·N·R·I

And what of the forgotten moments—those fleeting glances, the mundane routines? They, too, find refuge in memory's sanctuary. Perhaps they slumber, waiting for an external stimulus—a familiar melody, a sunbeam through the window—to coax them back into mind and heart.

Perhaps as Mary stared at the wood of the Cross, she found herself reminded of the wood of His crib, recalling the words of the angel Gabriel:

> Do not be afraid, Mary, for you have found favor with God. And behold, you will conceive in your womb and bear a son, and you shall call his name Jesus. He will be great, and will be called the Son of the Most High; and the Lord God will give to him the throne of his father David, and he will reign over the house of Jacob for ever; and of his kingdom there will be no end. (Luke 1:30–33)

She then sinks into these words and is reminded of her words of reply, "Behold, I am the handmaid of the Lord; let it be to me according to your word" (Luke 1:38). She looks upon her Son, the Word of God incarnate, fulfilling His Paschal mission with the salvation of the world as its fruit.

As Mary, full of tears, looks upon her Son, she remembers that kings came to worship Him when He was a baby. Mary held Him then as those kings prostrated themselves before Him and gave Him gifts. How did her Son go from being worshipped to being crucified? Long ago, Mary leaned over to kiss the God-Man, her Son; she now stands to kiss the wounds of the God-Man, her Son, our Savior. Any mother would understandably experience bitterness toward those who tortured and killed her child right in front of her. Yet, heroically, Mary's sorrowful heart instead enters into the mystery of her Son's words: "Father, forgive them; for they know not what they do" (Luke 23:34).

Mary "stands near Jesus" and consoles the heart of her Son. His consolation is her presence and the sense that she holds in her heart no bitterness but only the deep love of a mother without sin. He asks us now to console her.

In the Crucifixion narrative, the Hebrew translation for the word *saw* (John 19:26), is *ra'a*, which has multiple meanings, such as "observe carefully," "examine," "experience," and "discover." The Hebrew word indicates not so much what is seen externally but the grasping of the interior dimension of the heart. Jesus "sees" His Mother and asks her and St. John to "see" (behold) each other. Based on the deeper meaning of the words *see* and *behold*, Jesus asks them to contemplate each other and see each other in a completely new way; He is inviting them to embark on a new mission, a new "covenantal relationship." This new covenant establishes a brand-new relationship between Mary and the Church, as represented by the beloved disciple, John.

In the account of Creation, when God "speaks," what He says comes into existence; this is what Jesus is doing here. He is creating a new covenant, consecrating his Mother, Mary, to us, creating a new family. The working out of this new family unit is for John to establish a new closeness to Mary, taking her into his home, his heart, and his family life in every way as his Mother. Jesus is uniting two hearts in an intimate relationship: mother and son.

Many Christians today talk a lot about accepting Jesus into their hearts, but have we also accepted Mary into our lives as our Mother and said yes to our own role as her children? Have we "seen" this new covenantal relationship and received it into our own lives?

Bl. Bartolo Longo and the Sorrow of the Rise of the Occult

"In the name of the Lord Jesus Christ, I command you to look at the crucifix, focus on the cross." These are the words spoken by an exorcist priest to an energumen (a person believed to be possessed by an evil spirit) during the major rite of exorcism. The crucifix has always been important in defeating the devil because the crucifixion was the great victory over him. Why? Because the full maturation of God's love for man was revealed on the Cross—God's torn Son on the Cross. Satan is the antigod—he is antilove! His mission is to parody and destroy love. But Mary crushes the head of the serpent (see Gen. 3:15), and she does so with her heel at the foot of the Cross.

For exorcists in their work, chief among the many saints called into action, after Mary and St. Joseph, is Bl. Bartolo Longo. He will be an essential intercessor for us alongside Our Lady of Sorrows.

The story of this twentieth-century Italian blessed is not your everyday story. He was a fallen-away Catholic who became a satanic high priest. Still, through the devoted prayer of his family and through action taken by a close friend, he returned to the Catholic Faith, become a Third Order Dominican, and eventually built a great basilica to Our Lady of the Rosary in Pompei. Exorcists tell of his great power in overcoming the demonic and the occult.

First, a question: Should we be talking about the demonic and the occult? An exorcist priest who is a close friend of ours cautions people not to make dinner-table conversation about the devil a regular habit. Still, if there is good reason to engage in the topic, for such a project as this, we do so, but with an invocation to Jesus and Mary (which you are encouraged to do right now). As my priest friend likes to say, "Satan despises the names of Jesus and Mary."

We have spotlighted a sin or what leads to sin in each of the seven sorrows. Indeed, it is the ordinary work of the devil to tempt us to sin; sin is what gives Satan a foothold in our lives. In this chapter, we want to consider the rise of the occult, which is no doubt a consequence of sin.

Sin is the distance we have created between us and God—the distance from light. Theologically speaking, Satan lives in darkness—a darkness of his own creation. There's always a certain quality to the darkness around demons to protect them from the light because they must hide from light. The Dracula thing is right. Demons cannot stand the light—the light of truth, of beauty, and of goodness. They flee from it. So they must surround themselves with this strange darkness that consoles them and protects them.[108]

Two thousand years after Christ's victory, Satan and Hell are not more significant in volume or space; there are just more people willing to court Satan and all his empty promises. More sin equals less God, less God equals more darkness, and more darkness equals a rise in the occult—for in the end, the occult is man's reach for the divine without the help of the one true God.

The increased gatherings in Satan's name, the glorification and worship of satanic imagery, the exponential increase in the practice of witchcraft, and general adherents to the ways of paganism have become far too commonplace in our culture—this is all a product of the occult. The word *occult* means "what is hidden." In other words, it's a darkness you can understand only by entering.

[108] This is different from the darkness God made. God had made the darkness of night, but that's the darkness of enormous beauty because it's lit with different kinds of stars, the moon, and the beauty of quiet. Satan can only mimic, and he even mimics darkness.

In recent years, there has been an extraordinary growth in interest concerning astrology, spirituality, divination, and self-care mindfulness. But as Catholics, we must always heed these words of the Lord: "Do not turn to mediums or wizards; do not seek them out, to be defiled by them: I am the LORD your God" (Lev. 19:31). But those representing occult practices speak of "good" magic and of spiritual powers and paths apart from Christ that can bring about positive results in people's lives. This is, quite simply, not possible.

It falls to us as ambassadors of Christ in the world to pray for protection against such diabolical deceptions, as well as to intercede directly for those caught up in them. Tarot-card reading, which boasts a global market of more than a billion dollars, is a direct offense against God. If we know anyone who has fallen into the New Age traps of tarot-card reading, Ouija boards, and so on, we should warn those persons of the dangers of those practices and should be intentional in our prayer for them. Joined with the heart of Our Lady, we pray this sorrow for our protection against the demonic forces and the safety of our loved ones.

There are less obvious entry points into the occult as well, which we must respond to in the same way. Freemasonry continues to be on the rise and is quite serious. On the surface, it appears to be compatible with the Catholic Faith. It shows itself to be a fraternity rooted in truth and love. Freemasonry teaches a man to be righteous in civic duty and always to be honest with others. It also values brotherly love and conduct: such principles have always been important and can never become outdated. So why is Freemasonry incompatible with the Catholic Faith?

According to Leo XIII, Freemasonry adheres to naturalism, which is the idea that "human nature and human reason ought in all things to be mistress and guide." He adds that Freemasons "deny anything has been taught by God; they allow no dogma of religion or truth which cannot be understood by the human intelligence, nor any teacher who ought to be believed because of his authority."[109] As such, Freemasonry is a false religion! Furthermore, it has set out to destroy the Catholic Church.[110]

Freemasons are occultic, with their practices remaining hidden in the shadows. In each of the three levels of Masonry—always putting the "Lodge" above Jesus and family—the initiate must take an oath to conceal and never reveal the secret practices of the Masonic Lodge, otherwise subjecting himself to self-mutilation or gruesome execution. This is quite serious, as oath swearing lies at the heart of their faith.

In addition to Freemasonry, Wicca is another "shadowy" occult that has seen a significant rise. It is the largest, most influential form of nature-based modern paganism. Wicca picked up steam the early 1960s by environmentalists, feminists, and those seeking a nonstructured spirituality. Initially it was an underground movement, but commercial books about witchcraft published in the latter half of the twentieth century, along with television productions, created a surge of interest in youth and young adults. With the ability to find Wiccan communities online and the growing apathy toward organized religion, Wiccan witchcraft began its entry

[109] Pope Leo XIII, encyclical letter on Freemasonry *Humanum Genus* (April 20, 1884), no. 12.

[110] In the early twentieth century, while walking through St. Peter's Basilica, young Maximilian Kolbe came across a significant demonstration of Freemasons holding anti-Catholic, sacrilegious signs. In one case, a sign read, "Satan must reign in the Vatican / The pope will be his slave." St. Maximilian Kolbe encouraged every Catholic to defeat this lie by praying for the Freemasons. We are called to pray for those entrenched in this false religion. We have friends who are Masons, and we pray for them!

into the mainstream and has exploded in the twenty-first century. Like other occults, it holds its dark secrets with spell chants and blood rituals.

Dear friends, in the face of such diabolical activities and structures, we should turn with great confidence to Mary, who can provide a river of grace and who crushes the head of every heresy. Let us pray for all souls who are lost in the occult—especially for those close to us. Remember, our prayer does not change the heart of God but brings to fruition what is in the heart of God—the salvation of his beloved children!

In Jesus and Mary, we claim victory, and in Bartolo Longo, we find a rich companion to assist with that victory.

Bartolo Longo was born in 1841 in Naples, Italy, a time and place where Catholicism was increasingly under attack by Italian nationalists (some would have considered themselves Italian fascists). Intellectual circles at the time were not only anti-Catholic, but they mingled with the occult and Satanism—this was the social environment that young Bartolo stepped into as a student of civil law at the University of Naples. Bartolo was heavily influenced by the anti-Catholic sentiment and began to look elsewhere for his spiritual needs. He turned to Satanism, eventually becoming a satanic high priest.

Gradually, Bartolo would begin to experience the consequence of practicing Satanism. He started to suffer from depression, paranoia, and anxiety. The downward spiral and the irregular diet that was part of his occult practices affected his physical health as well. It finally took the influence of a close friend to pull him out of the depths of evil and into the light. This friend introduced Bartolo to a Dominican friar, who gradually led Bartolo to renounce his Satanist ways and come back to the Church. Bartolo returned to the sacraments and completely changed his ways, surrounding himself with Catholics, performing works of mercy, and becoming a Third Order Dominican.

Thirty years young, Bartolo traveled to Pompeii on a business trip that would change the trajectory of his life. While in Pompeii, he recognized the same indifference toward religion and the same entanglement with the occult that he had struggled with so intensely himself. It began to affect his spiritual life, but in a moment of deep prayer, he was reminded of the words that a Dominican once shared with him: "If you seek salvation, promulgate the Rosary. This is what Mary desires."[111] Upon hearing these words anew in his heart, he rose to action.

Promoting the Rosary became Bartolo's singular mission. It was not easy initially in the not-so-friendly confines of secularized Pompeii, but he did not despair. Putting his trust in Our Lady, he started a Rosary confraternity and began fundraising to build a church. To garner souls for Christ and generate enthusiasm and excitement for Our Lady and for his building project, Bartolo led catechism classes and Rosary crusades, and these eventually won over the hearts of the people. All of his efforts bore fruit, and in 1880, the Church of Our Lady of Pompeii, a Latin basilica, was complete. In time, it became a place of pilgrimage, and it was expanded in the 1930s to accommodate the volumes of pilgrims who flooded the church. In 2008, Pope Benedict XVI presented the basilica with a Golden Rose—a papal token of reverence that was first awarded in 1096.[112]

[111] "Feast of Our Lady of Pompei," Inside the Vatican, https://insidethevatican.com/magazine/culture/feast-of-our-lady-of-pompei.

[112] See Pope Benedict XVI, Pastoral Visit to the Shrine of Pompeii, October 19, 2008, https://www.vatican.va/content/benedict-xvi/en/speeches/2008/october/documents/hf_ben-xvi_spe_20081019_pompei.html.

If you pulled up a picture of a Satanist today, the very last thing you would think of is a saint. Yet that was Bartolo Longo. From Satanist to saint: the contrast could not be greater; that he was so far gone and yet was rescued brings home the need to draw souls out of evil's depths. The extremes are great, but the power of God is greater.

Bl. Bartolo Longo is in the heavenly court right now, waiting to be called into action. He knows the gravity of what the occult does to the soul and the anguish it causes Our Lady. He experienced both the extreme desolation of Satanism and the profound consolation of Mary's embrace—a consolation so profound that he dedicated his life to the cause of Our Lady in winning souls for Christ.

Bl. Bartolo Longo, pray for us!

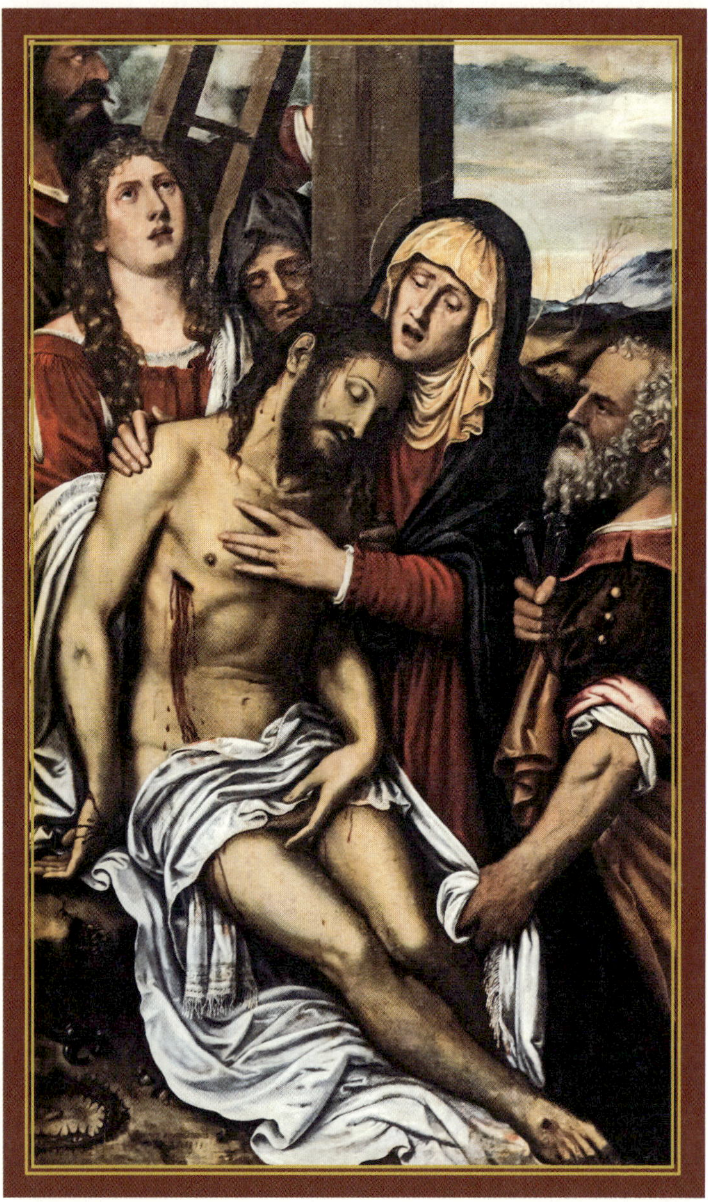

The Sixth Sorrow

MARY RECEIVES THE BODY OF JESUS IN HER ARMS

Matthew 27:57–61

When it was evening, there came a rich man from Arimathea, named Joseph, who also was a disciple of Jesus. He went to Pilate and asked for the body of Jesus. Then Pilate ordered it to be given to him. And Joseph took the body, and wrapped it in a clean linen shroud, and laid it in his own new tomb, which he had hewn in the rock; and he rolled a great stone to the door of the tomb, and departed. Mary Magdalene and the other Mary were there, sitting opposite the sepulchre.

Behold in silence this sorrow of Our Lady.

Reflection

Jesus' pain has ended, but Mary's begins anew. The lance pierced His heart; sorrow pierced hers. In His death, a piece of her also dies. She had known Him in His beauty and glory, but now she sees Him changed and deformed, bearing the weight of humanity's sin. Mary remembers Cana; the hour is upon her (cf. John 2:4), and it comes with great heaviness. Jesus performed His first sign at Cana by turning water into wine at Mary's request. Now she ponders the new wine in the blood that has just been spilled. She is "woman," the New Eve who will play a pivotal role in redemption.

There are two altars at the Cross. In the words of St. John Chrysostom: "Whoever then was present on the Mount of Calvary might see two altars, on which two great sacrifices were consummated—one in the body of Jesus, the other in the heart of Mary." Jesus' saving death bestows everlasting life, and Mary's heart, like an altar, bears the sacrifice of her Son. The Mother of Sorrows stands resolute, with her heart as an altar of love and sacrifice.

Jesus is taken down from the Cross and placed in the waiting arms of Mary, but she is not still. Her shaking arms reach for Him; she has longed to embrace Him, and now she can. She weeps, and the depth of her sorrow is revealed. We behold in silence the greatness of Mary's sorrow—the kind of sorrow that teaches us how to love, how to grieve. It is the *Pietà*—no words, just an image. Arguably, it is the most moving image in history—the image and point where all grief finds its consolation. Man has always been captivated by beauty, but this beauty haunts us, inviting us to consider the depth of sorrow, the depth of love.

Not long before this, Mary heard Jesus say, "It is finished" (*Consummatum est*) (John 19:30), and in her tears, she consummates the power of love, for tears are a manifestation of sacrificial love. "Jesus wept" because of the greatness of His love for His friend Lazarus when he died: "See how he loved him" (John 11:35–36). Mary now weeps because of the greatness of her own love. Like a coin with its two sides, love has two realities: joy and sorrow. Although we keep it at arm's length, death is the reminder that in a sense, sorrow "finishes" love—consummates love.

Certainly, the events surrounding Jesus' crucifixion unfolded rapidly. The Sabbath loomed, and time compressed. Amid the chaos, Mary, once standing, is now sitting, cradling her Son in a sea of tears. In that moment, time stands still, and the world fades away, leaving only her raw, unfiltered ache.

Imagine the weight of His lifeless body, the open wounds, the thorns still embedded in His brow. The weight—the heaviness—is not just physical; it's metaphysical. It's the burden of the echoes of laughter that will never be heard again. It's the silence that engulfs her, drowning out the cacophony of life around her. She held Him—this innocent Man, this Savior—knowing that time was slipping away.

But how long? How long did she have to hold Him? The minutes blurred into eternity. Perhaps it was mere moments, a heartbeat's worth of time. Or maybe, just maybe, the veil between Heaven and earth opened, giving the pietà its due time.

In moments of loss, we often grapple with the intensity of our emotions. The love we hold for someone or something shapes our experience of sorrow. It becomes a tapestry of memories, hopes, and dreams unfulfilled, interwoven with pain. Our Lady's sorrow, rooted in her love for her Son, transcended mere human understanding.

Her heartache was boundless because her love knew no bounds. Our Lady witnessed her beloved Son's suffering, Crucifixion, and death. The weight of that love pressed upon her, leaving an indelible mark on her soul. In her tears, we find solace—a reminder that love, even in its deepest anguish, is a testament to our shared humanity.

Mary passes through the misery of looking down upon her bloody, dirty, almost unrecognizable Son on her lap, a desolate mother with no proper burial plan for her Son. Mary was a poor widow with no other children to step in. She had been monetarily poor all her life, but she did what needed to be done with unwavering faith, trusting in God's provision for her. She now renews her prayer: "Let it be to me according to your word" (Luke 1:38).

St. Maria Goretti and the Sorrow of Our Hypersexualized Culture

"Blessed are the pure of heart, for they shall see God" (Matt. 5:8). Seeing is receiving, and the pure of heart receive God as He is and encounter that experience as God intended. The Immaculate Mother's pure heart receives her God and Son as He is taken down from the Cross—in all of His torn flesh—and takes in that moment as God desired. She weeps— not just as the Mother of God but as the Mother of all of us (see John 19:26–27).

Nearly two thousand years later, she continues to weep because of the gross impurities of man. God became flesh to redeem man. Man's duty is not to succumb to the temptations of the flesh but to offer each flesh-driven temptation to God.

If purity sees and receives, then impurity is blind and closed off. The world is increasingly closed off to God because it is stuck in the nasty filth of sexual sin—especially in the dark business of pornography. In this meditation, we will invite the powerful intercession of St. Maria Goretti to be a part of our Marian prayer to end the scourge of pornography and all its fallout. St. Maria Goretti will teach us to look into the face of sexual evil and claim Jesus over it. She will teach us that purity is strength!

The porndemic of the twenty-first century is no secret. Many articles and books have been published, highlighting this most heinous problem. Our most updated research found many staggering statistics illuminating its widespread impact. A study put out by *Psychology Today* compared the amount of Internet traffic to the three highest globally ranked pornography sites with that of several prominent digital media properties. Using various metrics, the authors found that the top three pornography sites are more highly ranked than the most well-known household-name sites, such as Amazon, Netflix, and Yahoo, as well as those that are the most up-and-coming: TikTok, OpenAI/ChatGPT, and Zoom. The numbers are jarring. In one sample alone, Xvideos, the top-ranked pornography site, had seven hundred million more total visits than Amazon, nine hundred million more than TikTok, and a staggering north of one billion more than each of OpenAI, LinkedIn, and Netflix.[113] It isn't easy to get your head around numbers like these.

What's more, people continue to find more ways of getting pornography in less detectable ways (file sharing, peer-to-peer downloads, and so on), and this makes keeping track of the money trail almost impossible. Given the sites trafficked, pornography is arguably the most lucrative money-maker in the world.

Globally, while young men make up the largest body of pornography users, pornography is a problem that touches both sexes and every age demographic. The numbers above point to the reality that we have morphed from a culture with a pornography problem to a culture that has enshrined pornography. This breaks Mary's heart!

Mary desires that we reclaim the practice of the beatitude of purity. In Matthew 5:8, the Greek word *katharos* can be translated as "pure," "clean," "without admixture," or "to be one thing." *Katharos* has a rich historical context. It directly alludes to the Old Testament Levitical priestly rite of purification. Here, the pure of heart are individuals who have not been corrupted by defilement or profanity but who possess a single-heartedness in their consecration to God. Essentially, purity guards "the intimate center of the person" (CCC 2533), drawing us deeper into the mystery of

[113] Nicole K. McNichols, "How Many People Actually Watch Porn?" *Psychology Today*, September 25, 2023, https://www.psychologytoday.com/us/blog/everyone-on-top/202309/how-much-porn-do-americans-really-watch.

God's life of holiness. To practice purity is to practice intentional offering.[114]

We must guard our hearts against the hypersexualization that has invaded our culture. On the personal level, if we fail, we must pick ourselves up and seek God's forgiveness, never forgetting that the first sinner Christ forgives in John's Gospel is a prostitute. Christ is aware of the struggle. We emphasize personal struggle because it always starts with the self. St. Francis of Assisi is believed to have said, "To sanctify oneself is to sanctify society." Before societies change, man must change. If the task is to be realized, Christ's gift of purity must first be actualized in our hearts and be the permanent condition of our spirit.[115]

Mary's grief extends beyond pornography to its damaging and horrific consequences: the rise in divorce rates and increased abortions.

As it has been observed, divorces are more likely to double among porn users. As a simulated act, pornography sterilizes and sabotages the natural gift of self intended for the conjugal act in marriage. When spouses are not loved but used, marriages devolve into utilitarian relationships. To paraphrase Pope St. John Paul II again: people are made to be loved and things used, but we use people and love things. Marriage is about loving our family and using things as their design orders.

Also, there is a clear link between pornography and the scourge of abortion. Pornography use leads to the increased demand for prostitution. Men who frequently use pornography are more likely

[114] It could be said that pornography is the icon of the devil (as it has been observed) because it is the great manipulation of the flesh-offering of Christ, which is the icon of Christianity.

[115] For a more detailed conversation on pornography, see Joseph Hollcraft, *A Heart for Evangelizing* (Steubenville, OH: Emmaus Road, 2016), 77–87.

to employ women in prostitution, which is to say that the demand for sexual services is influenced by exposure to explicit content. One can also intuit that higher levels of pornography use are connected to acceptance of abortion.

All these details should not leave us judgmental of those who have succumbed to pornography and its fallout; instead—as in each reflection on each sorrow of Mary—they should increase our conviction to be the intercessors that God is asking us to be, mindful that each of us is vested with the flesh and could just as quickly, without the grace of God, fall into impurity.

As we continue to pray for those in our circle of influence and the world, we do so with St. Maria Goretti, who teaches us how to overcome lust. St. Maria Goretti is unique in the canon of saints as she is one of the youngest canonized saints in the history of the Catholic Church. She died tragically on July 6, 1902, at the age of eleven.

She was born in 1890 in Corinaldo, Italy, the third of six children. When young Maria was nine, her father, Luigi, died tragically of malaria. It then fell to Maria's mother, Maria Assunta, to work the crops in the field while little Maria dutifully assisted her mother in caring for her siblings. Aside from caring for her family, she also had to cook and clean for her two next-door neighbors—one of whom was a man named Giovani Serenelli, who had a son, Alessandro. Giovanni took much of the profit from the farm, often leaving the Gorettis with little to eat and very poor.

During this time, young Maria grew in devotion to the Blessed Mother. She often frequented the Shrine of Our Lady of Graces, praying the Rosary regularly for the repose of her father's soul. She gained popularity in Corinaldo as the little girl who sold eggs and chickens and always smiled.

In June 1902, she began doing more work for twenty-year-old Alessandro. Alessandro was a large man who developed an impure desire for Maria. He said inappropriate and crude things to her, often making sexual advances on her that she would always resist. She did not tell her mother, for fear of causing trouble and losing money that would help the family.

On July 5, 1902, Maria attended to her daily duties, as she did every other day when Alessandro asked her to mend one of his shirts. She graciously said yes. As young Maria sat mending, Alessandro entered her room and motioned her into his bedroom. As always, she refused. This time, Alessandro grabbed young Maria and threw her into his bedroom. She refused to submit to him, and in a fit of rage, Alessandro brutally stabbed her fourteen times in the lungs, heart, and intestines. He left the room, and her family later found her with only a slight pulse. After multiple surgeries, Maria died the next day amid a horrendous infection brought on by her numerous lacerations.

Before her dying breath, her heart had one last thing to share with the world: "I forgive Alessandro Serenelli, and I desire that he come with me to Heaven. Pardon him, my God, because I have already forgiven him."[116]

Alessandro showed no remorse for what he had done and was sentenced to thirty years in prison. In his eleventh year of imprisonment (some have noted the correlation to Maria's age), Maria appeared to Alessandro. He claimed to see Maria walking in a garden, dressed in white, picking lilies. Joyfully, she came to him and asked him to accept the lilies. He took them, and as he held them, Alessandro said, they were transformed into a still white flame. Maria disappeared.

Alessandro's sentence was cut short by two years for good behavior. He served close to twenty-eight years. After being set free, his first act was to see Maria's mother and beg for her forgiveness.

[116] Fr. Jeffrey Kirby, *The Life and Witness of St. Maria Goretti: Our Little St. of the Beatitudes* (Charlotte, NC: TAN Books, 2015), 35.

When Maria Assunta opened the door, Alessandro asked, "Maria Assunta, do you know who I am?" Maria Assunta responded, "Alessandro, Marietta forgave you, Christ has forgiven you, and why should I not forgive you.... Your evil days are past, and to me, you are a long-suffering son."[13] Maria Assunta took Alessandro in and adopted him as her son. He lived by her side, eventually becoming a Franciscan lay brother and living out his days with a heart like a still white flame.

St. Maria Goretti's purity was her strength, and that strength, covered in forgiveness, transformed the crude, vicious Alessandro into the loving man of purity he became. Lilies are symbolic of purity; when Maria, dressed in white, offered lilies to Alessandro, she was offering him the grace of purity. He accepted. Alessandro was no longer carrying around a thousand pounds, the weight of a heart unreconciled to God. He was a man free from impurity, healed of his past wounds, and ready to abide in God. Incidentally, soon after Alessandro's visit from Maria, he requested a visit from the bishop. He confessed his sins.

Dear readers, as touched upon, we live in a very unholy, impure world. In this sixth sorrow of Mary, we pray for our protection against the wickedness and snares of impurity; we pray for the conversion of those we know who struggle with impurity. Meditating upon this sorrow reminds us of the importance of embracing our baptismal call to live in God and for others. We do this best by not holding grudges. Among other things, St. Maria Goretti teaches us that purity's action is forgiveness. Nursing grudges saps us of our strength and vexes us to no end. Let us keep in our hearts St. Maria Goretti's purity and forgiveness and our call to console Mary by being a people of forgiveness. Our prayer will be that much more potent if we follow the path of Corinaldo's crown jewel!

St. Maria Goretti, pray for us!

The Seventh Sorrow

THE BURIAL OF JESUS

John 19:40–42

They took the body of Jesus, and bound it in linen cloths with the spices, as is the burial custom of the Jews. Now in the place where he was crucified there was a garden, and in the garden a new tomb where no one had ever been laid. So because of the Jewish day of Preparation, as the tomb was close at hand, they laid Jesus there.

Behold in silence this sorrow of Our Lady.

Reflection

The Jews were unlike the other nations that surrounded them. The Mosaic Law prefigured the hope and eternal life the Gospel promises in its respect for the bodies of the dead. The reverence for what had been the earthly home of the soul of a loved one is seen in its precepts and ordinances regarding dealing with the deceased.

Mary is now facing her final sorrow and last responsibility toward her Son in preparing His body for burial and placing Him in the tomb. In this sorrow, she is finally physically separated from Christ. Even in this, she is not spared from fighting against time—Sabbath restrictions and prohibitions are quickly approaching, as are financial provisions for a tomb or a burial site. She must rely on the help of Christ's followers, not solely on her efforts, to provide for these requirements to be met.

This last sword of sorrow has mercilessly severed the last vestiges of that which Mary held dear and precious in her life. Simeon prophesied the sword of sorrow so long ago, and it has done its last and most painful work. "One thing after another," Mary experiences the final sword to the heart, sorrow number seven. Recall, the number seven conveys completion, holiness, and divine order in Hebrew tradition. The sealing of the tomb completes and brings to perfection Mary's "spiritual crucifixion" (a phrase used by Pope John Paul II).

What could possibly be left of her heart to suffer after this? Perhaps we might be led to believe nothing, because Mary's love was perfect in God, and love cannot know true perfection until it gives everything. Yet there is still more for her to suffer because she is now our mother.

For any mother, watching her son being laid to rest in the ground is a heart-wrenching experience. She feels a deep ache, as if a part of her has been torn away—because it has. Despite the emotional storm, she stands there, witnessing the final farewell. Her strength is both fragile and unyielding—a moment of raw vulnerability, when love and loss intertwine. She endures because she must—for her Son, herself, and the love they shared.

The amount we owe our dear Mother Mary is, at times, almost incomprehensible. The heroic way she suffered each blow to her heart during her own passion, is worth our earthly gratitude in perpetuity. Mary dispenses "grace upon grace" (see John 1:16), in part, because sword after sword pierced her heart.

It seems as if we could not exhaust the words to describe all the aspects of Our Lady's suffering: trauma, detachment, grief, separation, isolation, humiliation, desolation, rejection ... On the other hand, we cannot exhaust the treasures open to us when we meditate on her Seven Sorrows and ask God to inspire us with what we need to see inside each of those sorrows.

Everything Christ suffered, Mary willed to suffer. Why? For us. This is a key reason Christ asks us to entrust ourselves to her as His beloved disciples. And praying with Mary is not a duty but an honor and a privilege. Again, she is the New Eve stomping on the head of Satan.

Incidentally, a careful reading of this passage from John uncovers a nuanced detail of great importance. John's portrayal of the new tomb points to a new beginning. Located in the garden (Greek *kepos*), the tomb's newness is crucial to John's narrative. Biblical prophets often envisioned the forthcoming era of salvation as a new creation, reminiscent of the Garden of Eden. Ezekiel, representative of the redeemed, proclaims, "This land that was desolate has become like the garden [*kepos*] of Eden" (36:35).[117] John employs familiar images to explain the unfamiliar. The untouched tomb in the garden heralds the advent of a new creation, the Resurrection of Jesus. This biblical truth holds immense significance. Just as Eve's role in the garden of Eden was critical in the Fall of humanity, so is Mary, the New Eve, critical in the restoration of humanity. Mary, as the New Eve in this new garden, stands as the mother of sorrows—poised to push down on the head of the serpent as she waits for us to call upon her to release more graces!

[117] Francis Martin and WIlliam M Wright IV, *Catholic Commentary on Sacred Scripture: The Gospel of John* (Grand Rapids, MI: Baker Academic, 2015), 330.

St. Hildegard of Bingen and the Sorrow of Christ, the Good Shepherd

We are engaged in a battle that is unique in the life and history of the Church. While we know who wins, fighting to save souls is urgent. Will we fall victim to the spirit of the age, or will we cling to our Mother Mary, who, facing this last incomprehensible and infinite sorrow, continued to stand firm, steadfast in faith and in prayer?

There is a war raging for souls. Mary was pierced because she was and is in a battle. What saint do we invite into this meditation with Mary? St. Hildegard of Bingen, whose name means "battle." Indeed, this name was prophetic, as St. Hildegard fought for many things we take for granted today, not the least of which was speaking truth to those in her sphere of influence as a woman and a professed religious. In her writings, St. Hildegard of Bingen speaks in a very real way about a particular kind of wound afflicting the Church today.

The final contemporary sorrow we will consider here is a wound of shepherding in the highest places of the Church, frequently manifested in the abuse of authority, in sexual scandal, and in ambiguous teaching.[118]

The cause of this sorrow is not that the Holy Spirit has abandoned the Church and her shepherds, but, in some cases, the shepherds have have fallen under the intoxication of a hypersexualized and hypermaterialized culture and society. This kind of insidious atmosphere progressively diminishes the ability to pastor or teach, leading men who ought to be shepherds to become wolves.

[118] This contemporary sorrow and reflection on St. Hildegard of Bingen was the outgrowth of a series of conversations we had with Professor Anthony Lilles, Ph.D., Saint Patrick's Seminary, Menlo Park, California.

The role of the shepherd is at the heart of the life of the Church.[119] Jesus Himself said, "I am the good shepherd"[120] to make distinct the role of the priest as shepherd. Shepherds guide, lead, and care for the sheep by providing food, water, and shelter. Shepherds spend time with their sheep to build trust and familiarity. And of equal importance, shepherds must be vigilant, protecting their flocks from predators, such as coyotes and wolves. In the mind and heart of the Church, these coyotes and wolves manifest themselves in harmful influences (temptations) and false teachings. In writing to the Romans, St. Paul appealed to his brethren not to succumb to false teaching and to "watch out for those who create dissensions and difficulties, in opposition to the doctrine" that was handed on (Rom. 16:17; see Titus 1:9; Eph. 4:14; 1 Tim. 4:16; 6:3).

Hildegard was born to noble parents in 1098 in Bermersheim, Alzey, Germany. She became an oblate at the Benedictine Abbey of Disibodenberg at the age of eight and made her religious profession in 1115. At the young age of seventeen, she was a solemnly professed Benedictine. Hildegard's spirituality was deeply rooted in the Benedictine Rule. She practiced virtue with supreme generosity, guided and inspired by Scripture, the Liturgy, and the Church Fathers. Her obedience, simplicity, charity, and hospitality were especially evident. She sought to belong wholly to the Lord.

Around 1150, Hildegard founded a monastery in Rupertsberg, near Bingen, where she moved with twenty sisters. Later,

[119] The Latin term *pastor*, meaning "shepherd," is derived from *pastus*, a past participle of *pascere* "to lead to pasture, set to grazing, cause to eat."

[120] For an extended treatment on the richness and depth of this Johannine image, see Pope Benedict XVI, *Jesus of Nazareth: From the Baptism in the Jordan to the Transfiguration* (New York: Doubleday, 2007), 272–286.

she established another monastery on the opposite bank of the Rhine. As the abbess of both monasteries, she cared for her sisters' spiritual and material well-being, emphasizing community life, culture, and liturgy.

Hildegard actively strengthened the Christian faith and opposed heretical trends. Remarkably, she engaged in a fruitful apostolate, making arduous journeys to preach in public squares and cathedral churches across cities such as Cologne, Germany. In cooperation with the inspirations of God in her heart, she converted thousands to the Catholic Church. St. Hildegard's life exemplified holiness, originality, and dedication to God. She is celebrated as a mystic, a composer, an author, and a visionary. Her works include theological treatises, music, and accounts of her visions. Her insights expressed in poetry, medicine, horticulture, music, art, and prophecy were as unique as she was.

Throughout her life, Hildegard's gifted mind combined with continued private revelations from God to form the basis of a body of remarkable writings that can be regarded only as a singular gift to the Church. In one her most significant writings, Hildegard describes a vision of the Church as a bride standing before the altar in the sight of God:

> From her waist to the place that denotes the female, she had various scaly blemishes, and in that latter place was a black and monstrous head. It had fiery eyes, and ears like an ass', and nostrils and mouth like a lion's; it opened wide its jowls and clashed its horrible iron-colored teeth. And from this head down to her knees, the figure was white and red, as if bruised by many beatings; and from her knees to the tendons where they joined her heels, which appeared white, she was covered with blood.... The people who stood there,

> perceiving this, were shaken with great fear and said to one another, "Alas, Alas! . . . Who will help us?"[121]

In this vision, found toward the end of her three books of visions, Hildegard sees the Church suffering from an attack of the antichrist, a figure who opposes the gospel of Christ. The antichrist seems to be victorious in violently silencing the teaching and preaching of the Church. In our own day, when more Christians shed their blood every day, when the blood of the unborn is poured out without reprieve, believers can unfortunately find a very contemporary application of this vision.

In Hildegard's visions, there are five ages symbolized by animals: a fiery dog represents an age of angry people; a yellow lion, an age of warring and weakness; a pale horse, a period when virtue is neglected and fear takes hold; and a black pig, an age in which leadership is marked by boorish impurity. Finally, a gray wolf represents a time of the error of errors, when the sense of right and wrong is lost. Most interpret these ages as successive because they progressively describe the chaos over which the antichrist reigns.

Or perhaps they are simultaneous. All the animals seem present, but certain errors from Hell attack the Church in a way that she has never seen before, and the spiritual trauma manifests itself in a lack of conviction about truth and falsehood, the heroic and the cowardly, sin and grace. After relating this vision, Hildegard unpacks its

[121] St. Hildegard of Bingen, *Scivias*, Classics of Western Spirituality Edition (New York: Paulist Press, 1990), 493. *Scivias* is short for "Know the Ways of the Lord" and contains descriptions of visions that St. Hildegard contemplated for forty years before writing them down. She saw them constantly, amid her regular daily duties and even while conversing.

meaning through allegory. Her allegorical meditation includes this phrase: "And from her waist to the place that denotes the female, she has various scaly blemishes"[122]—"this is to say that, though she is now flourishing worthily and laudably in her children, before the time in which the son of perdition will try to perfect the trick he played on the first woman, the Church will be harshly reproached for many vices, fornication and murder and rapine. How? Because those who should love her will violently persecute her."

It is difficult not to extend this vision to the current state of the Church. We live in a time when the Church has been harshly reproached. If this is so, then we must also consider the reason indicated—namely, that "those who should love her will violently persecute her." Among those who ought to love the Church, those who are members of the hierarchy hold the primacy of place. Could there be among these also those who "should love her" but "violently persecute her"? This attack is so analogous to an earlier vision that it is difficult not to understand this image apart from it.

In an earlier vision, Hildegard perceived these followers of the devil as ripping children from the womb of the Church in a manner that possibly implies ministers who fall into sins of the flesh through abuse of the faithful:

> They are wicked fornicators upon themselves, destroying their semen in an act of murder and offering it to the Devil. And they also invade My Church with their schisms in the fulness of vice; in their shameful plots, they wickedly scoff at baptism, and the sacrament of My Son's body and blood, and the other institutions of the Church. Because they are afraid of My people, they do not openly resist these

[122] St. Hildegard of Bingen, *Scivias*, 495.

> institutions of Mine, but in their hearts and deeds, they hold them as nothing.[123]

Here, St. Hildegard suggests that those who hate the Church's institutions and work against them secretly are like "those who should love" the Church but persecute her instead.

An even earlier passage allows us to make this connection more explicit, wherein Hildegard admonishes priests who do not use the authority of their office to heal sin and calls them wolves:

> But if priests do not show the people the authority of their office, they are not priests but ravenous wolves. They hold their office by robbery as a wolf cruelly snatches a sheep, doing their own will instead of carrying the sheep. And because they live perversely, they are afraid to teach true doctrine to the people; they consent to iniquity as to a lord, for they harbor carnal desires, and they close the door of their heart to the helper as if to a stranger, for the justice of God.... How can you be their shepherd when you seduce them so? And how will you answer them when you cannot answer for yourselves? Therefore, weep and howl before Death carries you off.[124]

Here, the disturbing images of wolves and pigs are associated with the abuse of the priestly office. These are those who should love the Church but persecute her instead. Here, that persecution has the form of offering the Eucharistic Sacrifice in an unworthy way. In St. Hildegard's vision, this recklessness with divine things is a failure in pastoral charity—an absence of fatherly concern for the people

[123] St. Hildegard of Bingen, *Scivias*, 293.
[124] St. Hildegard of Bingen, *Scivias*, 285–286.

of God. Misery is always an absence of love, but this absence is a wound in the Bride of Christ that anticipates the fastening of the antichrist like a lion onto the womb of the Church. This misery is an absence of fatherhood, an absence of paternal teaching in the Church—an absence that allows the error of errors to come up from Hell and rob the world of all sense of right and wrong.

When we learn to weep over this absence of love in the Body of Christ, when we allow ourselves to ache over how this affects humanity's sense of hope, how it has robbed humanity of an understanding of the future, then the Holy Spirit can use our sorrow as He makes all things new. We can offer Him our sorrow so that the wounds of the hypersexualized and hypermaterialized shepherds in the Church may be transformed. We then share in Christ's mission to restore believers to health, helping them regain their footing on the firm ground of Christ, on which alone they can stand and find their way to the Father's house.

The Magisterium of the Catholic Church is a gift of the Holy Spirit to all of humanity. It is the power and authority to safeguard and promote the truth revealed by God. It is entrusted uniquely to the Holy Father and the bishops in union with him when they teach in the name of Christ's prophetic ministry in the proclamation of the Gospel. They can use this gift to explain how Christ's kingly and priestly ministries are to be understood and exercised. As a norm, the Holy Spirit guides the use of this power and authority when the minister intends what Christ intends. But the Bible also reveals (as does Church history) that such a minister can abuse his participation in Christ's prophetic ministry.

St. Peter illustrates the extent to which this can be true. Peter was uniquely entrusted by Christ with the ability to bind and loose within the Church, with shepherding in the place of the Good Shepherd, and with being the source of unity when all others who should be united have scattered (Matt. 16:16–20, John 21:15–17, Luke 22:31–32). Yet he is the same Peter who, when visiting the Catholics who lived in Galatia, succumbed to the temptation to avoid the conflict that comes from living and teaching the fullness of truth that his office demanded. St. Paul records that he had to correct our first pope publicly when Peter's actions brought about division and scandal, even though supposedly predicated upon a desire for peace and unity (see Gal. 2:11–14).

Against the confusion that St. Peter's error of judgment caused, St. Paul publicly and boldly admonished St. Peter to protect and safeguard the sacred truths of the early Church. St. Paul did this publicly precisely because Peter's weakness was also public. It is no secret in our own day that the papacy, even though instituted by Christ, can become a source of disunity and even scandal through ambiguous teaching and errant pastoral practices. As with Peter in Galatia, we might even affirm the presence of an authentic underlying desire to bring about peace, goodness, and unity—but when the methods of the world are employed to bring about the goals of Christ, it is Christ's own Body that is attacked rather than the true sources of suffering. The result is disastrous and so requires a firm resolution to cling to Christ alone when responding through both intercession and admonishment.

Those who hold the shepherding offices in the Church have a particular obligation before God to ensure the right use of this power and authority. The abuses that happen in the Church cause trauma that can take years, or even generations, to heal. Unfortunately, there is no shortage of examples of this in Church history. Thus, remaining silent regarding the abuses and ambiguities that offend Our Lord and Our Lady, simply hoping that the problems will go away on their own, fails to address the wounds inflicted on the Church and her faithful in the here and now.

Dear readers, in this seventh contemporary sorrow, we pause to consider an aspect of the current state of our Church's shepherds, because to all who have eyes, this wound is very real. It reflects a reality affecting many souls and grieves the heart of Our Lady. The proper reaction to this is not to accuse "the higher-ups" of grave sin out of righteous indignation but to react to the brokenness of the Church in such a way that we will intercede powerfully on her behalf. Only the brokenness of Christ on the Cross can heal the brokenness of the Church—this should be our prayer and not just our longing. The salvation of souls is at stake.

Through spiritual fathers who are faithful to their role as shepherds, the Bridegroom protects his Church and helps the world see what is right and what is wrong. Let us fervently pray for our faithful priests in this meditation and never stop praying for all priests to recover their identity as shepherds.

Hildegard of Bingen was truly a remarkable figure of the Middle Ages, but her influence is certainly not confined to that period. Her words of holiness and wisdom reached the heart of Benedict XVI, who canonized Hildegard of Bingen on May 10, 2012. On October 7 of that year, Pope Benedict declared her a Doctor of the Church in recognition of the impact of her teaching.

It is perhaps no coincidence that since 2012, when St. Hildegard became one of the Doctors of the Church, the Church has seen a particular attack—not just from outside but from within. In our series of contemporary applications to each sorrow, we have seen that Satan is plotting against God in subtle ways and not-so-subtle ways. We know who wins, but it is in entering into the wisdom of the mystics before us, like that of St. Hildegard, that we better contemplate the path toward our victory and the victory of Our Lady of Sorrows. Victory is found in the heart of the one who grieves!

St. Hildegard of Bingen, pray for us!

Appendix A

THE SEVEN SORROWS AND THE SACRAMENTS

Simeon's Prophecy / Baptism

The sacrament of Baptism changes us forever. In Baptism, we receive supernatural life in the form of sanctifying grace and a permanent mark on our souls that claims us as God's children. The graces that Baptism bestows were forged in the bitter sufferings of Christ's Passion and death. Neither He nor His Mother escaped the sword of suffering and sorrow, nor will we live in this world free from suffering and sorrow. Baptism incorporates us into the Mystical Body of Christ, and part of our participation in that Mystical Body is to share in the mystical suffering of Christ crucified. Our Lady has left us an example of doing everything, of finishing everything, that the law of the Lord and the Holy Spirit asked of her. In all her sorrows, she listened, obeyed, and persevered.

In the beauty and holiness of Joseph and Mary's presentation of little Jesus to God the Father in the Temple, an ominous bell rang out to all present. At Christ's first appearance in His Father's house, portentous words were spoken to Mary; in a sense, Simeon's prophecy to Mary also applies to each of us. In the sacrament of Baptism, we die and rise with Christ—this rhythm of dying and rising is repeated every time we conform our sufferings to the mystery of the Cross. The events of the first sorrow of our Lady at the Presentation of Christ in the Temple mirror our Baptism and entry into our Father's house and the dying and rising we do throughout our lives on earth.

The Flight into Egypt / Confirmation

Confirmation is a Sacrament of Initiation, establishing us as full-fledged members of the Catholic Faith. It is called *Confirmation* because, in it, the faith given in Baptism is *confirmed* and made strong (see CCC 1289). Confirmation "leaves its unique spiritual mark or character on the soul of the recipient"[125]—a singular grace whose effect is a maturing in the life of the Spirit.[126]

In Baptism, we—or our parents and godparents on our behalf—make promises to renounce Satan and believe in God and the Church. At Confirmation, we renew those sacred promises, internalizing them in heart and mind.

As we meditate on the Flight into Egypt, we are drawn to the feeling of uncertainty. The angel did not tell the Holy Family how long it would be until they could return home again but only to wait for another message. Like the Israelites, Mary had to live with her family in the desert for a length of time that only God knew. Do we not all have experiences in which we wander in a desert for what feels like an interminable time? How many times have we cried out to God in our prayers, "Where are You in my life?" Or maybe you have hit a rough patch in your life, and you wonder, "Will I ever catch a break?" The Holy Family also had this uncertainty, but unlike the Israelites, they put perfect trust and faith in God's

[125] Fr. Romanus Cessario, *The Seven Sacraments of the Catholic Church* (Grand Rapids: Baker Academic, 2023), 180.

[126] St. Thomas Aquinas, *Summa Theologica*, III, q. 72, art. 1.

plan for them, knowing that their time in the desert was for the greater good in the dynamic, unfolding plan for their Son.

In the end, made strong in Confirmation, we also are to be attentive to the voice of the Holy Spirit, to strengthen our trust-filled walk in God. Mary and Joseph "turned on a dime" upon the angel's prompting, and so are we to move swiftly at the prompting of the Holy Spirit, whatever the circumstances or the uncertainties.

The Loss of the Child Jesus in the Temple / The Eucharist

In the narrative of the Finding of Jesus in the Temple, there was no rest until Jesus was found; Mary and Joseph's pursuit of Jesus was pressing and urgent. We, too, should move with the same urgency to find Jesus in the Eucharist. In a certain sense, Jesus is lost to us if we do not receive Him regularly—every Sunday, at the bare minimum, or perhaps every day, if our schedule allows it.

In the Our Father, we pray, "Give us this day our daily bread." The Greek word for *daily* is *epiousios—epi*, meaning "super," and *iousios*, meaning "essence." In effect, the Eucharist is intended to be our "daily bread," the superordinary gift that is Christ—the essence of Christ. Nowadays, we hear the term *superfoods*, which refers to foods that nutritionists and health-care professionals credit with *preventing diseases of all kinds*, both mental and physical; these foods are said have healing properties that restore the body. The "superfood" of the Eucharist nourishes and restores the soul, *protecting it from all kinds of attacks of the devil.* We don't always see the immediate effects of the natural superfoods, but over time, we can see the impact of a superfood as the body heals. Similarly, while we might not always see the immediate healing effect of the "superfood" of the Eucharist, when we receive it in a state of grace we can begin to see the change taking place in our lives, over time, as Christ abides in us.

How does this relate to the loss of Jesus in the third sorrow of Our Lady? Our Scripture passage for this sorrow says, "Supposing him to be in the company they went a day's journey, and they sought him among their kinsfolk and acquaintances; and when they did not find him, they returned to Jerusalem, seeking him" (Luke 2:44–45). We often go along in our busy lives, assuming Jesus is with us because we possess "enough" of Him to have what we need. Instead, what we need is the frequent reception of the Eucharist.

What's more, just as Mary "pondered" the loss and finding of Jesus in the Temple, so should we ponder finding Jesus in the Eucharist if we are to grow spiritually and offer our trials and sufferings with Christ and Our Lady at each Holy Sacrifice of the Mass. Incidentally, during the Passover seder, the youngest child in a family had the important role of asking the question: "Why is this night different from all other nights?" The question encourages the gathering to discuss the significance of the symbols in the meal, pondering the meaning of the night as different from every other night. Likewise, we should ask: "What is the meaning of receiving the Body, Blood, Soul, and Divinity of Jesus Christ in the Eucharist?" The more we "chew" on what we eat, the more our praise of the divine indwelling will grow.

The Meeting of Jesus and Mary on the Way to Calvary / Confession

The sacrament of Confession is also known as the "sacrament of conversion" because it is "the first step in returning to the Father from whom one has strayed by sin" (CCC 1423). We can correctly walk with others only if we take the right "first step" with Jesus. Our steps to becoming saints are always measured against how seriously we take the first step in the sacrament of Confession.

At the center of a good Confession is a repentant heart. Repentance, like the Greek *metanoia* (change of mind), is a conversion of heart away from sin and toward God. This twofold movement of the heart is one of contrition and resolution. Contrition is "sorrow of the soul and detestation for the sin committed, together with the resolution not to sin again" (CCC 1451). Contrition is saying you are sorry to God the Father and meaning it from the depths of your soul. How often have we said "I am sorry" to a friend but have grown distant in that relationship without meaning it? On the flip side, how often have we said "I am sorry" to a friend and, meaning it, have grown closer to that friend? In other words, if we wish to heal our relationships, saying "I am sorry" must come from a place of intention—the heart. If we desire to advance in our relationship with Jesus Christ, going deeper in our spiritual life, we must say "I am sorry" from our hearts.

We show how much we "mean it" by doing penance. Penance is a way of saying "I love You" to Jesus, expressing your seriousness about Him as your close friend. We do penance to make amends for our sins and to be restored to complete spiritual health (see CCC 1459); full spiritual health is intimacy with Jesus; saying to Him "I love You!"

The sacrament of conversion is saying "I am sorry" and "I love You"—and meaning both! Out of one grief (our sins), we learn the language of another grief: the grief that is the sorrow and suffering of our loved ones and our neighbors. Jesus restores us in our sorrow, and as He does, He opens our hearts to walk with others in their sorrow. Love is an action verb—it flies to those in need. Mary loved Jesus by her presence, and she desires to teach us this art of accompaniment with others when we accompany her in her sorrows.

The Crucifixion / Anointing of the Sick

The Church gives us another type of healing through the sacrament of the Anointing of the Sick (see James 5:14–16; Mark 6:13). In this sacrament, a priest anoints the head and hands (or the feet of children) of the ill or the elderly. The grace of the sacrament provides strength and comfort to the sick and mystically unites their sufferings with Christ's Passion and death. The anointing is a sign of Jesus Christ's healing, for the soul and sometimes even for physical ailments. Many reported miracles have come from this powerful sacrament.[127]

Though the sacrament should not be limited to the time of death, it is often administered near death. Death should be a time of grace. The greatest gift given to humanity was through death, and our own lives should reflect that—our deaths should be gifts! What holds us back? Often, it is a lack of reconciliation.

In this fifth sorrow, the Crucifixion, we ought to be mindful of the beautiful grace of death, the moment in our lives when God calls us to our judgment. In this moment, Jesus exhorts us to forgive (see Luke 23:34), and He gives us the grace of the sacrament to push us forward in that direction. The Cross reconciles God with man, and so should our crosses at the hour of death reconcile us with man.

Our current cultural trend is pushing society toward morbid, anti-Christian end-of-life practices, not the least of which is the false "compassion" of euthanasia. It is never the right of man to determine the time of death; that is always up to God because, as only God knows the time and place of our death, He also knows the grace we need for our salvation. Death is a time of reconciliation, a drawing near to the hearts of our loved ones. Following the

[127] See Theresa Civantos Barber, "Amazing Story of a Cancer Cure through Anointing of the Sick," Aleteia, October 14, 2023, https://aleteia.org/2023/10/14/amazing-story-of-cancer-cure-through-anointing-of-the-sick/.

example of Our Lady, who stood by her loved One, we draw close to those suffering and accompany them to their eternal reward.

Mary Receives the Body of Jesus in Her Arms / Holy Orders

In the sixth sorrow, Mary experiences the crushing loss of her beloved Son. Our Lord's wounds and torn flesh lie open before Mary as she receives His body into her arms. What does she do? She cleans and dresses those wounds, as she had once tended to Our Lord by feeding, clothing, directing, and loving Him. This is what the priesthood does for us.

While observing that "at first glance," the Gospel is silent about Mary and the priesthood, Pope St. John Paul II makes an important point: "We know that Mary was present with the apostles who prayed 'with one accord' (Acts 1:14)" for the coming of the Holy Spirit.[128] Mary was most certainly present at the Eucharistic celebrations of the early Christians who were devoted to "the breaking of bread" (Acts 2:42).[129] As a "Woman of the Eucharist" for the entirety of her life, of course, she would be present in the first days of the breaking of the bread. As a mother, her greatest desire was to be with her Son, and the priesthood made that possible.

Mary's unique love for the priesthood is also one of consolation. The priest, through his ministerial service, shows us how to sanctify suffering and brings consolation those who suffer, especially Mary. Our priests unite the entire Body of Christ by healing and restoration "*in persona Christi capitis ecclesiae*" (the person of Christ,

[128] Pope St. John Paul II, encyclical letter on the Eucharist and its relationship to the Church *Ecclesia de Eucharistia* (April 17, 2003), no. 53.

[129] St. John Paul II, *Ecclesia de Eucharistia*, no. 53.

Head of the Church). To comprehend this, we must understand that sin, of any kind or degree, requires a ransom, a reparation. Only the sacrament of Holy Orders gives us that reparation. Mary's broken heart is united to the priesthood because the priesthood repairs what has been broken.

The Burial of Jesus / Holy Matrimony

In the context of Catholic teachings on marriage, the reality of "dying to self" holds profound significance. "Dying to self" refers to sacrificing one's desires, ego, and self-centeredness for the sake of a higher purpose or the well-being of others; it is not about extinguishing our individuality but about aligning it with God's will for the well-being of others. Jesus said, "If any man would come after me, let him deny himself and take up his cross and follow me" (Matt. 16:24). Essentially, it involves surrendering our own will and trusting that God's plan is ultimately best for us.

The failure to die to self and trust in God led to Adam and Eve's original sin. It remains at the root of all sin in some way or another. Being childlike (radically trusting) rather than childish (immature and self-centered) is essential for faithful discipleship within marriage (see Matt. 19:14; Luke 18:16). Certainly, the virtue of humility plays a crucial role in this process, as we learn to trust that God will truly fulfill us both personally and professionally. It's easier said than done, but Jesus is there to assist us in embracing this self-death (see Phil. 4:13) and experiencing His incomparable peace (see John 14:27).

In the sacrament of marriage, spouses are called to love and respect each other. They imitate Christ's sacrificial love for the Church through their sacrifices, joys, and faithful commitment. By dying to self, married couples witness the mystery of love revealed by Christ's sacrifice—His death and Resurrection (see Eph. 5:25).

Appendix B

LITANY OF OUR LADY OF SORROWS

Lord, have mercy on us.
Christ, have mercy on us.
Lord, have mercy on us.
Christ, hear us.
Christ, graciously hear us.

God, the Father of heaven, have mercy on us.
God the Son, Redeemer of the world, have mercy on us.
God the Holy Spirit, have mercy on us.

Holy Mary, Mother of God, pray for us.
Holy Virgin of virgins, pray for us.
Mother of the Crucified, . . .
Sorrowful Mother,
Mournful Mother,
Sighing Mother,
Afflicted Mother,
Forsaken Mother,
Desolate Mother,
Mother most sad,
Mother set around with anguish,

Mother overwhelmed by grief,
Mother transfixed by a sword,
Mother crucified in thy heart,
Mother bereaved of thy Son,
Sighing Dove,
Mother of Dolors,
Fount of tears,
Sea of bitterness,
Field of tribulation,
Mass of suffering,
Mirror of patience,
Rock of constancy,
Remedy in perplexity,
Joy of the afflicted,
Ark of the desolate,
Refuge of the abandoned,
Shield of the oppressed,
Conqueror of the incredulous,
Solace of the wretched,
Medicine of the sick,
Help of the faint,
Strength of the weak,
Protectress of those who fight,
Haven of the shipwrecked,
Calmer of tempests,
Companion of the sorrowful,
Retreat of those who groan,
Terror of the treacherous,
Standard-bearer of the martyrs,
Treasure of the faithful,
Light of confessors,

Pearl of virgins,
Comfort of widows,
Joy of all saints,
Queen of thy servants,
Holy Mary, who alone art unexampled,
Pray for us, most Sorrowful Virgin, that we may be made worthy of the promises of Christ.

O God, in whose Passion, according to the prophecy of Simeon, a sword of grief pierced through the most sweet soul of Thy glorious Blessed Virgin Mother, Mary: grant that we, who celebrate the memory of her Seven Sorrows, may obtain the happy effect of Thy Passion, who lives and reigns world without end. Amen.

—Pope Pius VII

ABOUT THE AUTHORS

DR. JOSEPH HOLLCRAFT is a Professor and Director of the High Calling Program at the Avila Institute. Dr. Hollcraft is the author of *A Heart for Evangelizing* (Emmaus Road, 2016) and *Unleashing the Power of Intercessory Prayer* (Sophia Institute Press, 2020). He has been featured on *EWTN Live* with Fr. Mitch Pacwa, S.J., and *Women of Grace* with Johnnette Williams. A former Catholic radio host, Dr. Hollcraft regularly contributes to multiple Catholic online journals and is frequently heard on Catholic radio airwaves discussing spiritual theology. Most importantly, he is a devoted husband and father. He lives in Canal Fulton, Ohio, with his beautiful wife, Jackie, and their four children: Kolbe, Avila, Isaac, and Siena.

RUTH BERGHORST, a devoted wife, mother, and grandmother, is a grateful convert to the Catholic Faith. As an accomplished author, she has dedicated more than a decade to mentoring young women in their spiritual journey. Her heart resonates with a special devotion to the Passion of Christ and the sorrows of Our Lady.

Sophia Institute

Sophia Institute is a nonprofit institution that seeks to nurture the spiritual, moral, and cultural life of souls and to spread the gospel of Christ in conformity with the authentic teachings of the Roman Catholic Church.

Sophia Institute Press fulfills this mission by offering translations, reprints, and new publications that afford readers a rich source of the enduring wisdom of mankind.

Sophia Institute also operates the popular online resource CatholicExchange.com. *Catholic Exchange* provides world news from a Catholic perspective as well as daily devotionals and articles that will help readers to grow in holiness and live a life consistent with the teachings of the Church.

In 2013, Sophia Institute launched Sophia Institute for Teachers to renew and rebuild Catholic culture through service to Catholic education. With the goal of nurturing the spiritual, moral, and cultural life of souls, and an abiding respect for the role and work of teachers, we strive to provide materials and programs that are at once enlightening to the mind and ennobling to the heart; faithful and complete, as well as useful and practical.

Sophia Institute gratefully recognizes the Solidarity Association for preserving and encouraging the growth of our apostolate over the course of many years. Without their generous and timely support, this book would not be in your hands.

www.SophiaInstitute.com
www.CatholicExchange.com
www.SophiaInstituteforTeachers.org

Sophia Institute Press is a registered trademark of Sophia Institute.
Sophia Institute is a tax-exempt institution as defined by the
Internal Revenue Code, Section 501(c)(3). Tax ID 22-2548708.